Career Hacks!

Easy Ways to Grow & Advance Your Career & Life

By

David Peters

Disclaimer

This book is designed as an information resource only and not as a definitive or specific plan for the advancement of any individual or specific career path. Every individual is different and every career and situation is different as well. Therefore it is not possible for the creation of one all-inclusive career advancement plan or process. It is the responsibility of the reader to determine the appropriateness of any and all parts of this publication and decide which should be used in their own situation. The writers, publishers, distributors and resellers of this book assume no responsibility for the use or application of any and all parts of this book.

Contents

Introduction

Everyone these days from the point where they get their first part-time job has ideas about what they want to do in life and the lifestyle they would like to have. In other words, they have a dream and need some way to help turn that dream into a reality. Some of these people will succeed while other may struggle. Sometimes the difference is not a lack of effort or a lack of knowledge, but simply not doing a few simple yet important things.

"Career Hacks" is designed to give anyone the skills and knowledge they need to give them a huge advantage over others when it comes to advancing their careers and getting more out of their job and life in general. This is important because the same skills and approaches we will use in advancing our career will also help us advance in life as well!

In this book you are going to find over 30 different things you can do to help you become noticed and appreciated more in the workplace. As you read this book you will quickly see that all of these things have one important thing in common. That is that they are very easy and require no special skills or abilities. So no one reading this book has an excuse as to why they could not do any one item in this book.

If followed, changing an attitude or approach to your life and career can be a very empowering process. Every change you make, every successful outcome you generate, helps make you stronger and more confident. This effect builds every time you create a success in your life and career. Success builds confidence and confidence helps build more success. It can be a powerful process for most people.

This book does its best to give you everything you need to get started making your career exactly what you want it to be. But it requires two things from you that we cannot provide for you. Without both of these things your chances of success are limited.

The first thing is honesty. In order to achieve anything you must be able to be honest with yourself. Some of these action items require you to ask certain questions of yourself as far as your skills and abilities are concerned. Do not try and convince yourself that you have skills or abilities that you don't have or that your skills are better than what they really are.

When you do that you are only fooling yourself. No one except you needs to know the answers to these questions so please be honest with yourself so you can take the required actions to get the best results possible.

The second thing is that you need to take action in order to make things better. We can give you all the knowledge and guidance and assistance we possibly can in this book but if you read it and never use it, the information will have limited value to you. If you want to get value and results from the contents in this book, you have to actually use it.

If you want a different result in anything in life then you need to change something. Very few things in life will change on their own and those things that do change on their own usually do not change for the better. If you want to lose weight and do not reduce what you eat or exercise more, you will not lose the weight. If you continue to do something the same way you are going to get the same results. When those results are not what you want, you need to change what you are doing.

Do not be afraid of change as change can help introduce new and exciting things into your life. Without change everything would be far too predictable and there would be little or no chance of improving one's life. So instead of fearing change as most people do, embrace it and encourage it.

Because that is how we take life and make it better. And that is also how we take our careers to the next level and make them better as well.

The topics and chapters in this book follow no particular order as far as importance is concerned. The truth is, how important each item is will depend on the person and their own particular situation might be. What might be critical for me might be almost useless for you and vice versa.

So go through the book and read each item. Try and see each item for what it is and how you might be able to use it in your life and your situation so you can get the results you need. If a particular item doesn't seem to apply, read through it anyway. Each item is only a few pages long and even though you might not think there is value in something you never really know. You just might pick up a new way of looking at something or a new way of thinking.

But whatever you read and whatever you decide, pick something and take action. Don't be afraid of changing something or trying something new. If it doesn't work out like you hoped or intended then change something a little bit and try again. Don't think of failure as failure. Instead, look at it as a learning process. Because sometimes eliminating something that doesn't work is just as beneficial as finding something that does work. It's just not as exciting!

So now that we have that all covered, let's get started!

Do Not Be
Good Enough

Before we actually start taking action and figuring things out, we first have to address a certain mindset that seems to be more and more pervasive within our culture. A particular mindset that is responsible for holding a lot of people back not only in their careers but in their regular life as well. Until we eliminate this mindset from our thoughts we will never reach our full potential.

The mindset I am referring to is the thought that being good enough to do something is all that is required. In more simple terms, many people believe that being good enough is good enough for them.

Here is the problem with that philosophy or thought process:

Opportunities often do not go to the most intelligent. Instead they go to the people who do their best to prepare for that opportunity.

That means being the most skilled, having the most impressive qualifications, the most relevant experience and being the overall most impressive candidate.

Some people believe that the requirements for a job or a promotion are all that is required and if you possess them then you are good to go without having or needing to do anything else. This could not be further from the truth. The qualifications listed for anything in your life or career are just the MINIMUM requirements for that particular opportunity.

Minimum qualifications are what you need to qualify for consideration for the job. Most people who have the minimum qualification are considered then quickly eliminated because what they have to offer is much less than what other applicants bring to the table. So unless the job has just one applicant, you, then you are likely to miss out on whatever it is you were going for.

If you want to have the best chance at succeeding or coming out on top when it comes to anything in your career or life then you have to change the way you think. Good enough should never be good enough for you. Good enough should be the starting point and you should build on things from there.

Whenever you set your sights on anything in your career, whether it be an opportunity that you know is coming your way or simply preparing for the next step in your career plan, you need to make a list of every qualification or relevant item and make sure you meet the minimum requirements. If you don't then do what you have to do in order to meet them.

But don't stop there. Once you have met the minimum, go down each item and determine what you can do to make every item or skill better, more impressive or appealing to the people who are the decision makers. Always try to give them as much of what they want as possible. Never settle for the minimum.

Your end goal should not be to achieve the minimum criteria for anything. Your goal should be to use the minimum criteria or qualifications as a STARTING POINT and then proceed to become as proficient and impressive in EVERY ONE of those items. Not slightly better, but as close to the best as you possibly can become!

You need to look at everything in your career for what it really is and that is a competition. A competition where everyone who wants that job, promotion or opportunity is going to fight for it against every other applicant. If there are 50 people applying for one job, those 50 people will be fighting each other for it.

Not with fists and kicks but with qualifications and performance. Different tactics and different weapons but it is a fight none the less!

Your goal should be to stand out from all the other applicants. But we want to stand out in a positive way. If our qualifications are poor but good enough, we will stand out in a negative way.

But if our qualifications are much better than everyone else we will stand out as a premier candidate and those are the ones who go to the next level or get that second or third interview.

It is easy to get complacent and believe that you have the skills necessary to do the job you are applying for or to be given that promotion that you wanted. But often times it doesn't make much difference whether you have the skills to do the job or not. If someone else has better skills, more skills, more experience, more education and other qualifications, THEY will be considered the better candidate.

There is one very easy way to stop yourself from being satisfied with your qualifications or performance. That way is to always assign higher goals and expectations for yourself than your boss or other people expect from you. This is a great way to go through your career because when your personal goals and expectations are higher than those that are expected of you, when you are satisfied with your performance that means others are bound to be thrilled!

For years I had a job where we had a zillion goals assigned to us. I created my own goals, which were higher and always committed myself to achieving those goals and not the company goals. When review time came around every year all my bosses and executives were far happier and pleased with me than I was with myself. So those reviews were always very positive.

This attitude does not only apply to getting a new job or a promotion. It should apply to EVERYTHING in your job or career. If people expect a certain level of performance from you, give them more. Don't work to their expectations, work to your own higher expectations. Don't walk out of a review or interview that went well and figure you can sit back and coast now. That's when you get into trouble.

I also want to give you one last thing to think about when it comes to where your skills and performance should be.

There will always be people in your industry that you either work with or at your competition that will always be looking for the same things as you. Assuming you all start out with the same qualifications, if you sit back and coast while everyone else improves their skills and performance all of a sudden they are at a higher level than you. So by doing nothing, you have in fact taken a step backwards because everyone else has taken a step forward. Realizing this can be a real eye opener.

So as you take steps to move ahead in your career, always try to do the following:

Try to take an existing skill and improve it.

Try to do something better and faster.

Take an older skill and update it.

Learn something new and apply it.

Always try to improve your overall performance.

If you can always focus on doing just those 5 things each and every day, you would be surprised how much easier and better your career will go for you. Doors will be opened for you and opportunities will be there that you are prepared to take advantage of.

This isn't magic and it most certainly isn't rocket science. What we will have is an attitude that will help us rise to the top over most other people and equip us to be ready for almost every opportunity that comes our way. Even those opportunities that we aren't totally ready for we will be much closer to ready than we normally would have been.

It's all about demanding and expecting more of yourself in everything that you do in life. If you can adopt this one mindset and approach, you will find your life and career moving forward much faster and a lot easier.

Life Is NOT Fair,
Get Over It!

Hey! I'm a pretty positive guy and I try to see the good in most everything but sometimes something will happen that just makes you scratch your head and wonder "How the heck did THAT happen?" We've all had this happen to us so this is not something unique by any stretch of the imagination. Since these things happen regularly, we need to learn how to react to them in the best way possible so we get better results in less time with less effort.

I'm not sure who stated the rumor that life is supposed to be fair but whoever it was, that person was dead wrong. A LOT of life isn't fair but the reality is that there are always going to be things that are out of our control and when those things happen, well, they just happen. We just have to understand that, learn from the experience and move on.

We have all applied for a great job, had really good qualification and then been passed over to see the job go to the owner's son or family friend. We've all had people go behind our back and get something we wanted by lying, cheating or stealing. It happens every day and again, all we can do is learn from it and move on.

We need to abandon this outdated and totally incorrect notion that life is somehow supposed to be fair and that good things are always going to happen to good people and bad things will always happen to bad people. It just doesn't always go that way and we need to accept that, understand that and do things that help put us in a better position to succeed next time.

That is where the problem lies in thinking we were somehow victimized when something wasn't "fair". When we think we were cheated or that something wasn't fair, we have two choices. The right choice, to accept it and learn from it so we are better prepared for next time, is the best and most efficient response. With this response we learn along the way so the same things do not happen to us over and over and over again.

The second choice is to blame others and complain about how we were cheated and that life isn't fair and blah, blah, blah. You know the response because we all have people in our lives who do nothing but complain how unfair something was but do nothing about it so they don't have it happen again.

The great thing about understanding that life isn't fair is that we soon become empowered. We no longer hide behind the "unfair conspiracy" and blame it for all our troubles. Instead, we take responsibility for what happened and we look for why things happened like they did and how we can protect ourselves the next time we are in this or a similar situation.

For example, if we are had a big presentation and someone stole your research and claimed it as their own before you had a chance to present it yourself, you can either complain about what happened or you can take steps to safeguard your work moving forward so no one would be able to steal it again.

Or when you go after a big job and lose out to someone less qualified you can either be annoyed and sulk or you can dig down to find out what that person had that you didn't or you can look for ways to make yourself look even stronger and more qualified next time. That is what successful people do. They learn from their mistakes and they learn from life. Then they use that knowledge to make reasonably sure they don't fall victim to the same things later on.

Whenever we hide between "fair and unfair" we often fail to accept responsibility for what happens. When we fail to accept responsibility for something we are far less likely to take action or make changes that will help us moving forward. Instead we blame others and do nothing until the same thing happens again in the future.

Notice I said "accept responsibility" and not "accept guilt". There is a big difference. You might not have been at fault when someone stole your work. So you would not admit or accept guilt but when you accept responsibility then you will ask yourself what you can do differently so they can't steal it again next week or next month.

I also see people say about other people "Boy were they lucky! They always seem to have all the luck!" This is their way of rationalizing why someone else was picked instead of them. Attributing everything to luck lets them off the hook as far as any responsibility is concerned. They might feel better but they learned nothing from the experience.

People who are lucky usually are known to have "made" the own luck. They take advantage of opportunities because they were prepared to do so. They worked while others goofed off. They made themselves look better while others made no effort to do the same thing. So their so-called "luck" was not luck at all. It was the result of doing the right thing and being better prepared.

As you move forward in your career, don't look for fair or unfair. Instead learn from your successes and your failures so you will be more prepared for the next time. Experience and responsibility are two of the greatest weapons we have in our success arsenal. We can either choose to use them or keep them locked away in the cabinet.

It's your choice.

Change on Your Terms

Now that we have all agreed that we need change and that change can be very good for someone's life and career, let's discuss how these changes can be made to come about. Because sometimes how change occurs is just as important and the change itself.

Change can come about because we want it to and we take actions designed to get that change to happen. This is often referred to as "pro-active" because we initiated the change and we did it in such a way as to make it easier to get the specific results that we wanted. This is almost always the best way to introduce change into your life.

Pro-active change is better because you are more in control of the entire process. You can do things on your schedule, on your pace and on your own terms. This allows you to control much more of what happens and how it happens.

This makes change easier and far less stressful. This is because it happens when you want it to and with your full knowledge and expectation. Little is left to chance and everything is well planned and thought out.

The other kind of change happens when something in your life changes on its own. That event or situation then forces change on you whether you are ready for it or even want it at all. Changes that occur this way are usually much more stressful and difficult to handle. You are at the mercy of the situation and often times cannot schedule different things easily into your life. Forced change is sometimes very emotional and difficult for most people.

The only good part about forced change is that sometimes the end results are better than when you started because that change really did need to happen in the first place. You might have never had the courage to make the change yourself but since you now have no choice, you just make the best of it.

An example of pro-active change is planning to change jobs and get a better job at a higher salary. Approaching this pro-actively would mean organizing your efforts to get the qualifications, updating your resume, researching jobs and opportunities and scheduling the entire process on your own terms when you have the time available. Then you can choose who you apply to, and field offers and make the decision as to whether to take the new job or not once you have the option and details in front of you.

That is something done at your own pace and on your own terms. Nothing is forcing you to do anything or make any change unless you feel that you want to. If the new job offer is not what you thought it would be you can always turn it down. Since you are already employed there is no financial pressure to accept the first job that comes along.

You can see that this is a far less stressful process since you are in control every step of the way and are not forced to do anything that you feel is not advantageous to you. You can pick and choose what you do and when you do it and only move forward when you are comfortable with the entire process.

Now let's look at the same example but with forced change:

You walk into work and are called into the manager's office. You are told that there is a layoff and that your job has been cut. You are told to clean out your desk, are given two week's pay as severance and you leave and go home. Now you have to make plans quickly because after the two weeks are up no money will be coming in and the financial pressure to take a job, possibly any job, can be substantial.

So you rush to get an updated resume out and because you don't have a ton of time to really perfect it and have it looked at by others, you put out a resume that might not be as good as it would have been had you had more time to do it.

You also can't afford to really search out jobs either so you mass apply for generic positions that might or might not be available or because the pressure is on you might even apply for jobs that are not better than the one you had. You might even apply for lesser paying jobs because of the financial pressure.

You go through interviews and your performance might be a little worse because of the pressure on you to find another job. You might appear desperate and your recent termination might also be held against you. Instead of dealing from a position of strength you are now dealing from a position of possible weakness. Don't think potential employers aren't aware of this and won't use it to their advantage during salary negotiations.

You might wind up taking a job offer you otherwise wouldn't have taken because you need the money. Once you are in your new job you can't start looking right away because spending so little time at a brand new job and then looking to leave doesn't look very good on a resume. So you stay for w while in a job you might not like at a salary that is less than you once had.

Those two examples of the same change show a drastic difference in outcome, stress and pressure. The pro-active approach was calm, organized and pressure free. The forced change was rushed, disorganized, frustrating and full of pressure. The pro-active change had a positive result of the change wasn't made. The forced change can have either a positive or negative result and we are not able to protect ourselves against it.

Every decision and every change we consider in our life and career is better when we do it pro-actively. Whenever we are in control and not pressured we are able to apply ourselves more efficiently and are usually able to go through the entire process in a more organized and focused manner as well. That means less stress, fewer mistakes and usually a much better and positive outcome.

This also applies to tasks and deadlines as well. If you know something is going to have to be done, then schedule it early and do it when you have the time to do it right and while you are not under pressure. Giving yourself time to do things on your schedule almost always has better results in less time as well. If something is due in two weeks and you have time in your schedule tomorrow, do it tomorrow. There is another powerful reason for doing this as well.

We never know what is going to happen tomorrow or next week. What we thought was going to be an easy week with little to do often turn out to be a nightmare week when something goes wrong or a last minute project comes your way. When this happens the last thing you need are left over tasks that also have to be done because you put them off. No one ever lost sleep because they had too much free time the next day but plenty of people have burned the midnight oil because of too many things to do and not enough time to do them.

Granted there will be times when things have to be done at an inconvenient time and not on your terms. That is part of life. But even in those instances when you can just worry about those things and not have a long list of other stuff that also has to be done, everything just goes smoother. You will also find yourself more prepared to handle anything that comes you way as well. That includes opportunities that you have already prepared yourself for.

Don't Hope, Do

Hope is a wonderful thing. It gives us the opportunity to see that life can get better and that the problems of today do not necessarily have to become the problems of tomorrow. Hope keeps us energized and focused on making things better instead of sitting back and allowing them to continue to be what they are.

But hope is only beneficial when we use hope in conjunction with proper responses to those thing that we have hope about. For example, if we have hope of getting a better job one day and we work towards getting the skills and education to qualify for that job, hope has done its job as an effective motivator. But if we cling to the hope of getting a better job but do nothing to help ourselves get that better job, then hope does not give us much of a chance for changing that hope into a reality.

How many times have we heard someone say "I hope I get that promotion" or "I hope I qualify for that mortgage" or something along those lines? Hope is one thing but most of the time we need to assist hope to make it reality.

If you hope to get that promotion and you work hard for it and prepare a great resume and practice to ace the interview, you might have a good shot of turning hope into reality. If you hope to get that mortgage and you worked hard to reduce your debt and raise your credit score, you might have a great chance of getting that mortgage.

But if you hope something will happen and then go sit on your butt on the couch hoping that hope is enough, you are going to have more failures than successes.

Hope shows us what could be and it is up to us to prepare ourselves to do whatever it takes to turn those hopes into reality. It is not a difficult concept to understand as long as you are the type of person who understands the importance of taking responsibility for what happen in your life.

Hope is wonderful and can be a powerful motivator. But hope only works when we take actions designed to get us where our hopes show us is possible. So have hope, take action and take your career and your life where you know it can go.

Don't just hope, do.

Appear Successful

This is one of a few chapters that is going to deal with how others perceive you. Though it is not fair, very often people develop perception about you that are not based on fact but rather their own interpretation. Sometimes these perceptions are favorable and sometimes they are not. But if you want to get the most out of life and do the best for your career, you are going to have to deal with all sorts of perception issues.

The first area we have to discuss is appearance. No matter where you are or what you are doing, you should always try to at least appear successful and confident. That means looking the part and playing the part. You do not have to dress up in a tuxedo to go out and get the mail but there are a few things you should be aware of.

Your Appearance Should be Appropriate for the Situation

How you look is going to change depending on where you are and what the situation is.

For example at work your attire might be business casual except on certain meeting days when you have to wear a dress or suit. But keep in mind that these are often minimum standards and you might want to dress a certain way even though it is not required.

Appropriate attire sometimes depends on your profession as well. You would not expect your auto mechanic to dress in a suit and tie and you would not expect your banker or financial advisor to wear jeans and a denim shirt. Both are acceptable attire for their specific occupation but not for the other.

You Want to Inspire Confidence

Your "look" should inspire confidence. It should make people want to believe in you and have confidence in your abilities. In other words, you want to look the part you are playing. When people look at you they should be thinking, "This person knows what the heck they are doing!"

Usually this entails dressing just a little bit better or looking just a little more comfortable or at ease in the situation. Maybe your dress or suit is a little better looking or your grooming just a little bit better. It is the little things that often make a big difference so pay attention to the details to create the look and appearance that you are looking for.

You Never Know Who You will Run Into

You can dress fancy at work and wear all the right clothes at the right time for the right people.

But you never know who you are going to run into when you run out for coffee Sunday morning in your "Screw the Establishment" t-shirt and ratty cut-off shorts.

This is not to say that you have to dress up like you are at work all the time. But keep in mind that everyone at work are people too and they don't hibernate in their houses until it is time to go back to work. They go outside to play. They go to restaurants and to the movies and to other things people do when they are not working. So if you would not be comfortable with your boss or the company owner seeing you wearing something, don't wear it outside. You never know who might see you.

What Your Appearance Says About You

Like it or not your appearance says a lot about who you are. Someone who doesn't take an active role in their appearance or who doesn't particularly care what they look like in public usually carries the same approach to the rest of their life as well. If they dress messy their home and desk are probably that way as well. If their clothes are dirty their personal hygiene isn't likely to be the best either.

Granted these are all stereotype and generalities but you always have to remember that perceptions are just as powerful as reality in a person's mind so if they look at you and draw a conclusion based on what they see, in their eyes that is who you are. Until you prove them wrong, that is what they will think.

What You Want to Achieve Through Your Appearance

Whether you are trying to impress your boss, co-workers, vendors or a prospective employer you want them to look at you and arrive at a positive opinion of who you are. You want your appearance to generate confidence in the eyes of others and not suspicion. First impressions are hugely important and since we usually see someone before we talk to them that first visual can make or break the conversation that follows.

When we give people what they expect, or whenever we give them more of what they expect, we stand a greater chance of having a positive interaction with them. Since it is always best to start off any conversation with a positive statement, and since we want to put the other person at ease, we should always try to have an appearance that places everyone at ease and speaks or competence and confidence.

So think of your appearance as the start of the conversation. Since we all want to give off a positive vibe or impression, it just makes sense to make the first thing someone sees about you as positive as possible. You can easily do that by being aware of what you are supposed to look like and what you do look like.

A Word of Warning!

For some people their personal appearance is very important to them and they feel that they should be able to look and dress the way they want whenever they want.

While this is your right, as long as it doesn't violate laws or company rules, keep in mind that other people are not required to share your views and can outright dismiss you based on your appearance.

So feel free to look like you want but also be prepared to accept the consequences of your choices whatever those consequences might be. Remember that we are trying to advance and build a career here. Not make a personal fashion statement to those at work.

Have a Plan

Ugh, I can hear everyone groan as they read the title of this chapter. After all, no one likes to plan very much and even fewer of us like to follow a plan after we are finished designing it. But the bottom line is that we need a plan so we know what has to be done and in what order things need to get done in. without a plan it is next to impossible to remember everything we need to do and what each items deadline is. So we need a detailed and accurate plan so we can keep our focus and get stuff done.

While we are not going to bore you with details on how to create your plan, we will give you several recommendations and important factors that should go into your plan. Remember that everyone is different so my plan might not look anything like yours and vice versa. That is why we cannot show you a good plan for you and why you must do this for yourself. We can help and we can advise but you must create your own plan.

Here are some things to consider as you create your plan:

What is Important to You?

Just like you wouldn't start out on a trip without knowing where you are going, you cannot possibly design a career or life plan without knowing your final destination.

There are several things to consider when it comes to where you want to go and it is best to give them thought now rather than later and have to switch paths and lose valuable time.

The first thing you need to understand is what is important to you? Remember this is your personal plan and it should reflect getting more of what is important to you into your life. This plan is yours and no one else's so it makes sense that it be customized for you by you.

So write down a list of those things that are important to you. Include such things as family, values, the type of career you want, the amount of time you feel you can dedicate and anything else that you need to factor into your plan as you design it. All of these can be changed later at any time but for you they show you your final destination and the path to take to get there.

What Do You Want to Achieve?

This is your basic end goal. By that I mean where you hope to be once your plan is complete. It can be one item such as "Earn $250,00 per year as CEO" or it can be a few things such as wanting to get a specific job, live in a specific place or any other objective that can be identified. Whatever your goals are in life and career, list them now so you can build them into your plan.

This is important because your objectives become constant reminders that will help you stay on path. For example, let's say one of your goals was to have time to enjoy your children and family. With that goal in your plan, you are more likely to set aside time for family activities because you see that goal. If you find yourself working 9,000 hours a week with no time for anything or anyone else, when you look at your plan you will see that you are off track as far as that goal is concerned. Then you can make whatever changes you see fit to get back on the right track.

What Kind of Career Are You Thinking Of?

You don't have to have a specific job in mind as you create your plan. Sometimes we are not even aware that certain jobs even exist until we are offered them or they are made known to us. But we should at least have an idea of what kind of career we are interested in. Do you want to be a writer, an engineer, a doctor, a salesman, a scientist or a teacher?

Knowing what you want to do will help you focus your time and energy towards that particular path and help you keep focused. Your career choice or industry can change at any time as you become more aware of yourself or as your attitudes and priorities change. But for now, we need to know which direction to start off in to help get us started.

Naturally, you should be picking your career and not your parents or grandparents or anyone else.

You can listen to them but always remember that this is your plan and it should be based on YOUR decisions and never someone else's.

What Kind of Education or Skills Are Required?

Early in the career process we should have a pretty good idea of what type of education is going to be required to qualify you for a job in your chosen industry. It might be college or trade school or it might require an advanced degree. You might be able to get started in your career with a college degree and then add an advanced degree as you move up the ladder to more advanced positions.

Understanding educational requirements now can be very useful as it gives you an idea of the time and money it is going to require to get you started. If you don't feel you can afford the expense, or if you feel that a college education is not something you are capable of for any reason, it is best to know now so you can readjust your plans or look for other alternatives.

Keep in mind, however, that there are many plans and programs out there that are designed to make college affordable so do not let money stand between you and your dreams. But excessive debt is not good either so you should understand this going in so you can make the right decisions.

Do I Already Have What I need or Do I Have to Get Them?

Any time we look to get into something new, there are bound to be qualifications. At this point we want to match up our qualifications with the qualifications of the job or industry and see what we already possess and what we have to work towards. This will help us develop a realistic timeline as far as where we want to be at any given time in the future.

This also helps us prioritize what we do so we can get the most important qualifications addressed first so we stand the best chances of success. This can also help identify weaknesses as well so we can strengthen those things to make us look better to others. Remember that getting a new job or moving up the corporate ladder is a competition and having the strongest skill set and experience helps a great deal.

What are the Steps Required to Get Where I Want to go?

Chances are your plan is not just getting a job and remaining in that job for the rest of your life. There are probably stages to your plan such as getting one job, working towards the next job and so on until you reach CEO or whatever your end goal might be.

Understanding the steps required is important because qualification usually get more in-depth and more difficult as you move up the ladder towards the better and higher paying jobs.

Not only that but as you move up experience plays a more crucial role in getting those jobs and experience takes time to get. So being able to identify now what you will need later can give you a huge head start on getting the experience you need to move forward.

What Are the Desired Time Frames for Each Step?

Part of a plan includes time frames for each part so we know whether or not we are moving in the right direction and at the right place. Time is important because if you hit your dream job at 40 that is much better than hitting it at 65 when you have 2 months until retirement! So assigning a time frame to each step allows you to plan not only your advancement but the preparations for the next phase of your plan.

For example, if you are in one job and in order to get the next one you need to get an advanced degree, then the time required to get that degree would factor into your timeline. If the next job in the company requires 5 years' experience in the job you are in right now, that would factor in as well.

All of these time frames can be changed at any time as conditions or situations require. But at least you will have a pretty accurate timeline to follow and prepare for. This isn't a perfect or exact science but it will help you stay on track and let you know what needs to happen and when.

What Has to Be Done in Each Step?

We spoke about each phase or step of our plan having different and perhaps more stringent requirements. So now that we know where we are going and the various steps in our plan, we need to understand what needs to happen at every step so we can make sure we are prepared for every step as it approaches.

Basically all we are doing is creating a "to do list" of everything that needs to be done so we can do them on our own schedule without the pressure and stress caused by doing things at the last minute. We already discussed the benefits of doing this so creating this list is important to the overall success of our plan.

How Can I Measure My Success or Progress?

With any plan, you need ways to measure how effective your plan is in helping you achieve your goals and also to measure whether you are ahead of schedule, right on track, or behind schedule.

If you look back at what we have done so far you will see that we spent a lot of time and energy going over time frames and different tasks and the order in which those tasks need to be done. This is all designed to add one very critical component to your career plan. That element is organization.

An effective action plan is an organized blueprint on how to get from where you are to where you want or need to be in the most direct and efficient manner.

It will also be able to let you know at a glance where you are as compared to where you are supposed to be. This will enable you to either achieve your goals faster or make corrections to get yourself back on track and move in the right direction.

Specific time frames are important because we need to see very easily where we are so we continue to do the things necessary to keep on track and on the right pace. Specific dates, deadline and the ability to measure different parts of our plan enable us to more closely monitor our progress or lack of as the case may be.

This means assigning time frames and specific goals at critical points in your plan. For example, step one needs to be completed By July 1st and step @ by September 1st and so on. The more specific your goals are the more likely you will be to complete them and complete them more accurately.

For example, "take a class in web design" might be an action item but it is not very specific or measureable. But "take a class in web design by September 1st and have my first site online by October 1st" is more specific and had specific deadlines.

Don't be afraid of goals or intimidated by them. They are there to help you and can always be adjusted when legitimate reasons are encountered. But goals also keep you motivated and let you know when what you are doing is not as effective as it should be. In other words, goals help you get on track and stay on track for longer periods of time.

Summary

This is not meant to be a complete and definitive lesson on how to complete the best possible action plan. Entire books have been written on this subject and it can be an interesting subject to learn more about. So much of life requires action and knowing how to create an efficient and accurate action plan is a skill that will come in handy often.

So take a class, read a book or just practice and refine your own plans as you go. You will find your efforts will be rewarded by enabling you to achieve more in less time with less wasted time and efforts. It can never hurt to become more organized and efficient!

Model Your Behavior
& Approach

No one knows everything about everything in life and most of us learn though our personal experience which unfortunately usually means that we learn from our mistakes. While there is nothing wrong with learning from one's mistakes, there is another and much more beneficial way of learning through mistakes.

That is learning from someone else's mistakes!

Some of the most successful people in this world got that way by trying new things, learning from their mistakes and refining their approach until they found something that really worked well for them. By modelling our approach and behavior based on what has already been proven successful we can learn what not to do and what to do without losing time and resources.

So it makes sense to try and identify the top producers or performers in your particular career or industry and learn as much as you can about them and their story. Very often they will have gone through pretty much the same processes and problems that you are going through and you can see what they tried. You can see what worked and what didn't work and you can create your own action plan based on your new knowledge.

Even though everyone is different and there is no guarantee that what worked for someone else will also work for you, reading or talking to people and finding out what they did might make you try something a little differently or alter your approach and save you a lot of time and hassle. This usually results in your reaching a particular achievement or goal faster because of less wasted time and efforts.

Learning can be a unique experience because sometimes learning what doesn't work is as important, or possibly more important than what does work. Successful people learn from both their successes and their failures because the lessons we learn from our failures have a lot of value as well.

Ask yourself what you would rather do. Try 10 different approaches to solving a problem and getting it right on the tenth try or sitting down and reading the 10 different approaches and finding out which was the right one before you got started? You can get it right the first or second time or you can get it right the 10th or 11th time. Which do you think is the best way to proceed?

Another reason to seek out the advice and life stories of others is that there is usually more than one path to a specific goal or objective. Sometimes the best path for us might be the one we are not aware of. Enlisting the help or advice of others might help us become aware of these other paths early on in the process.

There is a myth that most super successful people are just extremely smart and knew what to do from the very start and did everything right and moved straight to the top. The reality is that most successful people worked damned hard and made a lot of mistakes along the way that made them better businessmen or better engineers or better at whatever they do for a living. They too those mistakes, learned why they were mistakes and then changed their attitudes and actions so they could move on.

I'm sure the first computer program that Bill Gates wrote did not make him a billionaire and the first computer that the Apple founders created did not work perfectly either. But they had a dream, they made their mistakes and they ultimately become successful. Aren't these the people you might want to learn more about so you can get help achieving your dreams?

Do yourself a favor. Pick out one or two people you admire or respect in your career path or industry and learn about their history and back stories.

Chances are you will learn a few things that will help you avoid some of the mistakes that they made. After all, it is better to learn from the mistakes of others than it is to make those same mistakes yourself.

Have Goals

This is the first of a few "quick hitters" to help you achieve your goals in a faster and more effective manner. Don't confuse a short chapter with an ineffectual topic. Sometimes things are so important that you just don't need a lot of words to deliver the message!

In this chapter we are going to continue our discussion on the importance of setting a few goals along the way to your objective. Goals not only help us get and keep focused but they also allow us a quick and easy way to confirm that we are where we need to be at any given time. When we are falling behind, they can also help us hear a few "warning bells" along the way as well.

The difference between a hope or dream and an objective is a goal. Hopes and dreams are just what they imply. They are things we want but have little idea what is entailed in order to make them a reality.

Goals, on the other hand, when properly designed not only give us a roadmap and an organized route but also help establish the right time frame so that everyone that needs to get done is done on time so everything else can proceed without delay.

In order for a goal to be a good goal, it has to be a SMART goal. By that we mean a goal should be:

Specific – smart goals are accurately defined and very specific so there is little left to doubt or interpret. A well-crafted goals make it very easy to understand what is involved and how it will happen.

Measureable – A smart goal is a goal that can be measured. It is not subject to interpretation or emotion. In other words you cannot "think" you accomplished something, you will have real and factual data to confirm whether you did or didn't accomplish that goal.

Achievable – smart goals are goals that are not over ambitious and are, in fact achievable. For example, losing 5 pounds in 30 days is an achievable goal. Losing 20 pounds in one week most certainly is not. Having goals that are considered achievable will help keep people engaged and motivated.

Results focused – smart goals are focused on getting the right results. In other words, achieving the goal will help you get towards your goal and will become an integral part of your success. This, and your overall goal will help keep you engaged in the process.

Timely – smart goals ALWAYS have a time frame attached to them. Without a time frame a goal is not really a goal. If you need to lose 20 pounds for health reasons and you manage to do so but take 40 years to do it, did you really achieve your original goal or did taking that long really undermine the reasons behind the weight loss? Getting something done and getting it done on time are equally important in many situations.

Taking this one step further, taking large goals and breaking them up into "minim-goals" helps keep you motivated and engaged because you achieve these "mini-goals" faster and progress is more easily recognized and demonstrated.

For example, if you have a goal of losing 100 pounds, that might seem very intimidating to most people. They might get so intimidated or overwhelmed that the overall task seems so large and so unachievable they might quit altogether. But taking that 100 pound goal and breaking it down into 10 – 10 pound goals or even 20-5 pound goals will help people see their total progress more easily and help keep them engaged in the weight loss process.

It really doesn't make much difference how you utilize your goals or how you set them. The important thing is that you get the results you want within the time frame you want and that is precisely what setting goals enables you to do.

Your goals are also your business and unless you decide to there is no reason to share your goals with anyone else unless that person is part of the process. Your successes or failures are your own business and no one else's so if it helps to keep your goals to yourself then just do it. But take those goals seriously and do your best to live up to them and achieve them. If something gets in your way once in a while you can change your goal or your timeline but only when you have a legitimate reason to do so. Do not just change a time line when you are lazy and fall behind.

Remember when you cheat or try and dodge the system the only person you are cheating is yourself. And don't you deserve better in your life?

Have Ethics

Anyone who has picked up a newspaper or listened to a television newscast knows that ethics seem to be taking a back seat to just about anything in today's society. But that doesn't mean you should dessert them as well because ethics are still highly valued by most businesses and people these days. You just don't hear about those people in the newspapers.

Over my 40 years in the working environment I have seen many people whose ethics are seriously missing or in question. The one thing almost every single one of these people had in common was that they eventually were discovered and ultimately failed. The failed because their focus and activities on the way up alienated so many people and destroyed so many relationship that they were just not able to recover and stop the rapid fall that ultimately came.

I watched a business owner who routinely abused his employees and played with their careers and life with no regard whatsoever.

I watched his business fail as good people either were fired or left for better working conditions. There were few tears shed for him when his business went under.

We have also seen people bend the rules or blatantly disregard them all in the name of making a sale or getting ahead only to find themselves on the wrong end of a lawsuit or spending years in prison when what they had done finally caught up to them. In the end, those who cheat or steal in order to get what they want usually do not go unpunished.

At certain times we might be tempted to skirt the rules or take a shortcut to get us where we want to be by taking advantage of someone else or acting in less than an ethical manner. If you find yourself in the situation we have one very important piece of advice for you.

Don't do it.

Your personal reputation takes years to build and can be destroyed in a matter of minutes if what you did is discovered and made public. If you steal someone else's work and take credit for it in order to get a promotion or some other award, you run the risk of having your credibility destroyed and lost forever.

If you lie and cheat your way to the top there will always be a whole bunch of people who resented the way you rose to the top and they will be only too happy to hasten you fall. If you cheat your way to the top, don't expect a lot of friends or a lot of hope on the way back down. You wouldn't deserve it and you are not likely to get it.

The best way to achieve any goal or objective is to do it openly, honestly and with integrity. Ask yourself if getting that job is worth your personal reputation or integrity. Hopefully you will tell yourself no. But risking everything that you spent your life building and creating is not a smart decision. There is just too much at risk to take the chance.

Instead, take the high road. Base your rise on your hard work, your treatment of other people and your skills and attitude. Work with others to achieve things not against them so you get all the credit. I am not saying that you should be a doormat for anyone looking to take advantage of you. But don't allow yourself to cheapen your standards or throw away your values because everyone else is doing it.

Because even it might seem that way, everyone is not doing that. You just don't hear about those people. But they are out there and those are the people you should model, not the others.

Have Passion

They say if you are doing something you love for a living that you never will actually work a day in your life. I am not so sure that is 100% true but the fact remains that if you love what you are doing you will do a better job and have an overall better attitude when it comes to doing your job and getting the best results.

One thing that other people often look for in a co-worker or worker is whether or not they have a passion for what they are doing. In other words, for that individual is it just a job or is it their life's passion? Do they truly love what they are doing and take pride in their work or is it just a way for them to earn a paycheck and pay the bills?

I had several jobs that I enjoyed and did very well at and I was well respected for my performance as well. But when I started writing my first training manual I soon realized that I would write for hours and it seemed like it was only minutes!

I could sit at my typewriter (yes, I used them way back when) and I would write and I would lose all concept of time. As life went on there would be times when my wife would walk into my office and ask when I would be ready to go to dinner and I thought it was still morning or early afternoon!

THAT is what happens when you truly enjoy something or have a passion for it. That is what people look for when they need someone to entrust with a special project or to hire for a new or better position. No one wants someone who treat their job as just a job. No one likes to hire a "clock watcher" or someone who is only looking to do as little as possible in order to get through the day.

Those people have no passion and it really shows. They might look great on a resume but when they get in front of someone or have their first day on the job, the truth really comes out and comes out fast. These are the people who can never get ahead in their own company because their co-workers understand who they really are. These are the people who constantly go from company to company because they look f=great on a resume even though they are nowhere near as great in person.

I really urge you to find something you can earn a living at that you really have a passion for. Something that resonates within you that you can embrace and take pride in. Even at just 40 hours a week you will spend over 2,000 hours a year at work. Shouldn't you want to spend those 2,000 hours doing something you are passionate about?

Sometimes we may have to make a choice between doing something that we are passionate about and something that pays more money. Sometimes this can be a very difficult choice especially when financial pressures really make you need to earn more money just to pay your bills.

But sometimes taking a lower paying job doing something you love can result in more rapid growth because others can see your passion on display every single day at work. You will quickly become someone known for their work ethic and attention to detail and someone who can be trusted to do a great job even on a moment's notice.

All because you are doing something you either love or that means something to do. This is precisely why some people work for charity or cause instead of a higher paying job. I cannot make your mind up for you but I do strongly urge you to choose a job or career that you can be passionate about. Something that will make you excited in the morning to go to work and something that will make the hours of the day fly by instead of watching the minute hand creep around the clock all day.

Sometimes we don't have to be the smartest or the best at what we do as long as we have the passion and fire to do our best. Many people recognize this and choose the people they believe are the best fit for the job. So place yourself in the position to do something you love so that love and passion can convince someone to give you a bigger and better job in the future just because you have that passion.

Become an Authority

Every industry or company has certain people they value because of their overall knowledge about their products services or their market segment. These are those people they go to for information, advice or opinion. Since much of this information is not learned through any school or course but rather through personal experience, those employees are particularly valuable to the company.

These are those people who have come to be known as "authorities" in their particular area of expertise. Often times these people are the only ones with particular knowledge that could be useful in resolving problems or handling disputes. In other words, these people have the knowledge and abilities to get things done and get them done right.

Since these are highly valued people they are also highly sought after as well.

So the questions really should not be "Should I become an authority" but instead "HOW do I become an authority"? The answer to that question is that you start gathering knowledge and practical experience so that you become one of the most qualified people in your company or department.

The problem might be finding or discovering that particular knowledge because like we said above, this knowledge is usually not found in a seminar or class. It is usually practical information garnered through first-hand experience or field work. In other words, you've been there, done that, and got the t-shirt.

Actually living through something and experiencing or doing it is quite different. There are a LOT of people chocked full of book knowledge but little practical experience. I personally know some people with engineering degrees that could tell the difference between an adjustable wrench and a cheese sandwich. But they can design something using their book knowledge.

Actually the best way to become an authority is to read everything you can get your hands on and talk to the people who are involved with these things day in and day out. While we mentioned that seminars usually do not teach this kind of information the other people who go to these seminars often possess it and are more than willing to share it. Sometimes you learn more during the lunch break by sitting down and having lunch with these people and talking to them than you learn in the entire seminar.

Just getting their name and phone number to add to your contacts can prove valuable for both of you. Don't use lunch as a rest period. Take advantage of it.

Never pass up an opportunity to listen to or talk to people who are actually doing what your company is interested in. find out their little "tricks of the trade" or "field hacks" as some people call them can prove very valuable and insightful to people when they need them. Just knowing these things, or at least knowing where to get the information when it is needed can make you very valuable to others.

One other reason for becoming known as an authority is that people tend to listen to people who have that reputation a lot more carefully and tend to believe what they say a lot more. This is because as an authority you have almost instant credibility in their eyes. They figure that someone with all that knowledge and all those contacts surely must know what the heck they are talking about.

Getting ahead in your career or life is all about getting people to recognize you and pay attention to you. When you develop an audience of people who trust you and listen to you it is possible to do great things and accomplish great goals. And when it comes to building and growing your career, things don't happen in a vacuum. The things you do and how people feel about you often play a major role in what happens next.

Last, but certainly not least, on a selfish note, increasing one's knowledge and improving one's performance is a great way to get noticed as being someone who is worthy of a better job, higher salary or at the very least, the grudging respect of your co-workers. All of these factors come into play when it is decided who gets the next promotion or who keeps their jobs during an upcoming lay-off.

Always keep in mind that your worth to the company lies in your knowledge, your work ethic, your commitment to the company and your ability to provide the greatest value to the company and your co-workers. Someone who is well known as an authority, who can be counted on to provide the answers or resolve a situation, has a huge, often virtually unlimited, value to the company.

So start today gathering information and knowledge. Add to your list of contacts and develop internal and external sources for the information you don't have but might need in the future. This is important because although you might not know everything it is often just as good to know where to get those things you don't know.

So do your best to become known as an authority in your area of expertise. Set yourself above everyone else based on your knowledge and performance. You don't have to outwork everyone else and you don't have to schmooze anyone to get ahead. All you need to be is you, the authority, and everything else will soon fall into place.

Become the "Go to" Person

In addition to becoming known as an authority, you also want to be known as the person to come to whenever there is a problem or situation that needs to be resolved. You want to get the reputation as someone who can be trusted to do anything when asked and is able to do the job right and to the best of their ability.

Think about the people you have worked with over the years and which of those people you thought highly of and which of them you were not overly impressed with. Chances are you were impressed with the people you could rely on and upset or angry with those who seemed to sit back and be happy to let everyone else do the work.

People who want to rise up the corporate ladder usually have to demonstrate their skills and work ethic in order to be chosen for higher paying and better positions within the company.

Those people above you, the usual raid to work and also has the skills and attitudes required to get the job done. People who show these characteristics are the ones that rise through the company faster than others.

The process for becoming a "go to" person is actually quite straight forward. It might not be easy at times but it is very straight forward. Here are a few ways you can earn a reputation as a go to person:

If you see something that needs to be done, do it.

If someone asks for a volunteer, then volunteer.

If you can help someone, then help them.

If you are asked to do something, do it yourself and do not look to pawn it off on someone else.

Don't hide from work or make excuses as to why you cannot do something. If you can do it then just do it.

You do not want to get the reputation of someone who tries to avoid work all the time. You know the type. The employee who always manages to disappear when the boss is coming so he won't have to volunteer for something. (This person is also usually the one who has to use the restroom just as the waiter is coming with the check!)

People who take this approach are often disliked by their co-workers because their work load is increased because they are not carrying their fair share of the workload.

Adopting the attitude of a "go to" person has many advantages. It places you in a better position to be noticed by management and those above you because you are frequently volunteering to go above and beyond and do things other people normally wouldn't do. If the quality of your work is great, then being noticed by those above you is a great way of getting an advantage over a promotion when it comes around. As I already stated, management loves people who do good work and are not afraid to work hard.

Doing more than expected is also appreciated by your co-workers as well. There is a certain amount of work that needs to be done and the more work you do the less that is left for everyone else. Since most offices or groups are overworked as it is, anything to make the lives of co-workers easier is usually much appreciated.

When you volunteer to help others you quickly get the reputation of being a "team player" which others appreciate as well. As long as you are not constantly taking all the credit or placing yourself above everyone else, people will appreciate the help because your efforts help them look better as well.

Though we will discuss this in more detail later, "go to" people are also known as problem solvers and this is a skill that is highly valued by just about everyone. People who always seem to find a reason why they can't do something are a dime a dozen. But the person that will constantly look for solutions instead of excuses are those who are highly thought or and highly valued.

Who would you like to work alongside in your job? Someone who always is there to help or someone who is always looking for the easy way out?

I thought so, me too.

Become a Problem Solver

Ok, we just explained why it is important for you to become known as a "to do person" and also establish yourself as an authority in your area of expertise or industry. The two are different yet closely related and they all address a concept that is at the center of why anyone is hired for any position.

No matter what you do or what your job is, there is one reason why you were hired for that position. That reason is that you have the skills, knowledge and ability to solve a problem. That problem is the reason your company has someone in your position. Without a problem to be solved, there is no reason for you to be employed in the first place.

A newspaper needs stories and information to publish so they hire reporters and writers to provide that information. Stores need someone to ring up purchases and accept payments so they hire cashiers. Stores also need people to help answer questions and select the best products for their customer's needs so they hire salespeople.

The list can go on and on but the bottom line is that everyone is hired to address a problem or a need and once you understand that, the process of making yourself more valuable and sought after in the marketplace is easy.

Because you are employed to address a need or solve a problem, then approaching your job and career in that manner will help you do more of the things that people you work with and those above you will appreciate. It is not like you are likely to do anything that much differently. You will just be looking at your career a bit differently, that's all.

Since this is a book about getting more success into your career and advancing your career in the best and fastest way possible, let's look at things from the advancement point of view and how becoming a problem solver will make you more attractive and desirable to management. Once we understand this then we can easily position ourselves so that we are in the best possible place when the next opportunity rolls around.

Think about the hiring or promotion process for a moment and place yourself in the position of the interviewer. Not only is he or she going to want the most skilled person for the job, they are also going to want the person who will take care of the most problems so the people above that person will not have to deal with those problems. If you were the boss or manager of the person that is going to be hired (and they are almost always part of the interview process) would you hire the best problem solver or would you rather hire the person who would wind up causing you more work and headaches?

99% of the time the manager would hire the person who would make their lives easier and better.

If you don't believe that, think about the workers in your own life. Do you like the person who always gives the headaches to you instead of taking care of them for you or do you like the person who always leaves those situations up to you? If you are honest you will admit that those people who solve problems are the most valued and trusted employees.

With all that in mind, why not start today looking at everything from the point of view that you are there to provide a service, address a need and solve a problem. Do not stop until you have achieved those goals. Upper management and those around you are bound to notice that everything is running smoother, everyone is a lot happier and that you are capable of handling every problem or issue and at the same time providing valuable leadership as well.

Several years ago I was a field manager for a very large company and my boss called me up and told me he was going through his escalation folder of all the territories that made up his division. There were 8 territories so he had 8 segments to his escalation folder. As he went through the folder he soon realized that every territory had pages and pages of escalated issues that he had to get involved in. My territory page, though, had none. Not a single one. And the reason for his call was to just say thank you for making his life easier.

So you might not think that people notice some of the things that you do or realize the value of the support and efforts you make. But trust me many people will realize and they will appreciate having you on their team. And when it comes time for a promotion and you need a reference from your manager, you can believe that it is going to be a very good reference.

Be an Effective Communicator

There are a lot of people out in the workforce that are highly skilled and have a ton of experience. While some of these people go on to have successful careers and earn the respect of others at the same time, there are others who seem to have their careers stalled at one point or another and they never seem to be able to move on. That is sometimes because though they mastered their job and the skills required to do that job but they neglected to strengthen or master other important skills.

One of the most important skills that anyone can have in any industry or any field is the ability to communicate effectively. It is amazing how many people are employed in leadership and management positions that are absolutely terrible at communicating with others. This not only hurts their own productivity but the productivity of everyone else as well.

Though there are entire books and courses available on how to communicate properly and effectively, we are going to give you the basics in this chapter and they should be enough to at least get you thinking about how you can communicate better with others and make you aware of a few things that you might not have ever considered before. By the end of this chapter you will at least become more aware of the importance of communication skills and can decide where you need help and where you can get it.

Here are the most important aspects of the communication process and how they can effect your career:

You Need the Ability to Speak Clearly

Part of the communication process is being able to speak clearly so that other people are able to hear what you have to say with very little or no effort. Sometimes people have a tendency to mumble or they talk with a heavy accents making it difficult for people to hear what they are saying.

Every time someone does not hear or understand what you are saying that opens up the possibility of them trying to guess or draw their own conclusions which may or may not be accurate. This can result in wrong information and wasted time and resources when people do something that is different than what you intended.

You need to be Able to Be Understood Easily

Being understood means more than speaking in a clear voice that is free of accents or inadequate volume. Also important are the words we use and the way we present the material we are trying to provide to others. If the message is there but we deliver in such a way that people do not understand it, then we have failed to communicate effectively.

For example, if we are talking to non-technical people and we are explaining things using highly technical language and terms, people might not understand what all those terms really mean. It might be OK to speak to engineers and technicians in that manner but not anyone else. That means that we have a responsibility to know and understand who we are talking to and to choose our approach and delivery carefully and appropriately.

It might also mean speaking a little slower to give people a chance to hear and absorb what you are saying. It might also mean taking a break at regular intervals to ask if anyone has any questions and confirm that everyone understands what has been discussed so far. The earlier we can correct misunderstandings or fill in gaps of understanding the better off everyone will be.

While some people believe that it is up to the person listening to make sure he or she can easily understand what is being said, the reality is that the speaker also share in this responsibility. This is important because some people will never let the speaker know they don't understand and this creates even more opportunity for confusion and poor judgment.

You Need to Provide Enough Detailed Information

Good communicators leave little to chance. They don't just tell someone what to do they tell them how to do it, when to do it and in some cases, where to do it. If you have a message to get across or directions you want followed, you have to be as specific as possible so you get exactly what you want when you want it.

If you are teaching or explaining something to someone you need to not only give them the information they need to understand but also specific examples to make it even clearer. You have to assume people don't know anything and give them everything they need even at the risk of boring other people who do know those things.

The more information and details you provide the less people are going to have to think about or assume. The result to this is getting more of exactly what you are looking for and less wasted time and resources. All of this adds to improved productivity and less stress in the office or work environment.

You Need to Know How to Listen

This is one area that many of us don't even think about. We think we know how to listen but the harsh reality is that a lot of people have no idea how to listen properly. They think they do but they really don't. This can be difficult to explain to those people as well.

Listening requires not only listening to the words being spoken but also the tone and emotions in those words as well. By listening to the tone and emotions we can gauge how important something is and also the emotional state of the person speaking those words. In many cases these additional areas of listening will be more important than the actual words being spoken.

In fact, it has been estimated that less than 20% of what we communicate to other people is contained in the actual words that we speak. The rest of the message is contained in our tone, our emotions and the gestures and body language we project as we speak. As listeners, if we fail to "listen" to all of these factors we run the risk of totally missing the message or the importance of that message.

Another part of listening that many people fail in is the ability to concentrate on what people are saying. Many people feel they can text their friends, watch their computer monitor, read the newspaper, watch television, do their e-mail and a host of other tasks at the same time they are listening to what someone has to say.

The fact is, the more things we try to do at one time the more difficult time the brain has allocating resources to each of those tasks. If we are listening while typing an e-mail for example, we might only be using 33% of our brain power in listening while the rest is used in typing and reading and thinking about that e-mail.

Sometimes when trying to do more than one thing at a time we will often "zone out" and become so engrossed in the other task that we might miss huge chunks of what the other person is saying! This can have significant effects on our ability to understand the entire content of the conversation.

Make no mistake about it, if you want to listen effectively you have to pay attention and give your total attention to what you are listening to. Put down the cell phone, turn off the television or monitor and just listen. Trust me, you cannot do multiple things at the same time and do a good job with them all. Some things are going to suffer and listening and comprehension are usually some of them.

Another factor of multi-tasking while listening is when you are face to face with someone and listening to what they have to say. When you are listening while e-mailing or doing something else you are showing disrespect to the other person and this is rarely taken well by most people. You are in fact telling them that what they have to say is not worth your time to listen. Think about that the next time you feel the urge to multitask during a conversation.

You Need to be Able to Write Effectively

Communication is also important when it is done in non-verbal form. Being able to write clearly and effectively makes it easier for people to understand what you are writing while also remaining engaged enough to actually read the whole letter or e-mail through to the end. Since skimming over letters and e-mails is something most people do and can lead to misunderstanding and poor comprehension, we need to provide incentive for people to read what we write.

In a business setting, clear and concise is important. In other words, if you can deliver an accurate message or point in two paragraphs, do not take 4 pages to do the same thing. Everyone is busy and no one really has the time to read through a long winded accounting of something that could have been explained in a few sentences. Respect other people time and keep it short and sweet.

Try and also write with a little bit of flair and style so your e-mails and letter do not come off dry and boring. I'm not saying you have to be a stand-up comedian but make it enjoyable to read what you have written. Again, it is better for everyone if people read what you have written all the way through.

Deliver your message in an easy to read format that is enjoyable to read while giving everyone all the information they need to properly understand what you have written.

Write it using words that most people will be able to understand and right to the audience you are writing to. Make your content as specific and relevant to the reader as possible. This will help them remain engaged and also help them realize that this actually does apply to them and that they will benefit by taking the time to read it.

Always remember that anything you put in a letter or e-mail can become a permanent record so do not write anything that you would not want anyone else to read and make sure your content is appropriate and not offensive. Not everyone has your values, morals or sense of humor so be careful what you write so it doesn't come back to cause you problems in the future.

Last, but not least, remember that what you write and how you write it reflects on you. Make sure your spelling is correct and your choice of words is proper and appropriate. You never know who might wind up reading your content and they often will form an opinion of you based on what you have written. So be careful.

You Need to Command the Respect of Others

As a communicators, getting people to listen to you is extremely important. However, people who don't respect you or feel that what you have to say has little or no value are not likely to listen to you at all. Since this will impact your ability to communicate and get your message across accurately, you need to take steps to gain the respect of those you are communicating with.

In this book we have discussed a few ways to get people to respect you and look at you in favorable terms. Most of these items revolve around trust, integrity and work ethic. They also involve how we treat and interact with other people and how we conduct ourselves in the workplace. These are all important factors when it comes to the communication process as well.

Always treat people with respect throughout the communication process. Do not talk down to people or ridicule them in the presence of others. Make conversations non-confrontational whenever possible and make it easy for people to contribute and voice their opinions. Depending on your position in the group there might be times when you have to assert authority over others but limit those times so people do not feel as though they are being dismissed.

On fallacy regarding respect is that you can demand that people respect you. That is most certainly not the case. You can demand that people do things and follow your instructions but you cannot demand respect. What you CAN do is gain the respect of others through your actions and behavior and treatment of other people. You can show them that you are someone worth listening to and someone who knows what they are talking about. That will eventually lead to respect as long as you continue to earn that respect.

You Need to Accept TOTAL Responsibility for the Entire Communication Process

This last item sometimes makes people a little bit angry but it is something everyone needs to understand regarding the communication process. I have heard some pretty knowledgeable and well known people say that the communication process is a 50-50 partnership between the speaker and the listener. That each person has an interest in the process.

While I agree that the process is a partnership I do disagree on the 5-050 part. I believe that the responsibility for the communication process is not 50-50 but instead it is 100-100% where all parties have total responsibility over the entire process. Not partial responsibility but full and total responsibility.

If you are talking and I cannot hear you I need to make you aware of that. But at the same time you should make sure that you can be heard by asking if the other person or people can hear you. That is an example of both people taking ownership of the entire process.

When one person takes ownership, or when one person takes ownership of just their part, strange and bad things can happen. Using the example above, suppose the person listening can't hear very well but says nothing and the person speaking doesn't ask if they can be heard? What happens then? The message doesn't get delivered effectively and misunderstandings are more likely to happen

One person might be hesitant to speak up so the other person needs to make sure on his or her own. This is the only way the entire process has the best chance of succeeding. That means leaving nothing to chance and everyone involved assuming total responsibility for the entire process. If we are just concerned with our part, we are leaving fat too much to chance.

Keep in mind that the entire communication process is a results oriented process. When things go well we get the results we need or want. When things don't go so well we enhance the chances of misunderstandings and wasted time and resources. So it makes sense to take care of the process and continue to be aware of the parts of the process and your role in it.

This is not difficult and learning how to communicate effectively and easily will not only help you in your business and career but in the rest of your life as well. Most relationship problems stem from communication issue and most confusion in life occurs because someone could not deliver his or her message properly to someone else. So whether you are the speaker, writer, or listener, remember it is your responsibility to make the entire process go as planned. If someone is wrong, speak up. If something isn't understood. Ask questions until it is understood. Do you part and make sure everything goes as planned so you can get the results you want each and every time.

Be Positive

For some people this one will be a piece of cake while for others this just might be the hardest thing in the whole book to conquer. As a rule, people like to be around positive people and in the workplace this tends to be even more true. In a business environment people who are negative are not looked upon fondly by others in the company.

We have all worked with the person who constantly finds fault with every little thing and is quick to point out everything that is wrong while having little or no ideas as to how to make things any better. This can drain the life out of an office and poison the entire team. No one like to have an 8 hour complaint fest every day of the work week.

While nothing is perfect and while there are things that can and should be changed or made better, the fact is a lot of what we do throughout the week must be done within the system. So it really doesn't do much good to complain about something once the problem is made known to others. By that I mean if you think something is wrong, make your feelings known and have discussion but then don't obsess over it.

If you want to be looked at in a favorable light then keep the negative comments to a minimum. If something is wrong and you have an idea how to make it better then voice your opinion and share your ideas. That is how change usually comes about. Change does not come about by just complaining. It comes about from action.

Positive people inspire others to be positive and develop positive attitudes as well. They help create a happier and more productive work environment and they are much easier to work with as well. It is no wonder that most of the people who rise the fastest in their careers are the ones with a positive "can do" attitude.

Sometimes this is easy when the office atmosphere is positive in nature. But if the company is a difficult company to work for or when they make extreme demands on their employees that can make it difficult to remain positive. Then there are the employees themselves. If you work with positive people, it is easy to change your outlook to a positive one as well. But if the people you work with are all negative and complainers then it might be almost impossible to be the lone positive person in your group.

Being positive does not mean that you have to find everything in life perfect and become a giant ray or sunshine in the office. No company is perfect, no staff perfect and no day goes by with everything being perfect either.

So being positive isn't about living in perfection or demanding perfection, it is about carrying a positive attitude through everything whether the situation is positive or not.

Some people might refer to this as "seeing the silver lining" or some other well-known phrase, but being positive just means not dwelling on the negative aspects of life and instead looking for the positive parts of even the most negative things. Usually, if you dig down deep enough, you can find something at least partially positive in most things. Positive people grab onto the positive parts and move on from there.

The one key part to positive people, and why they are so respected and in demand in almost any company, is that they tend to be able to get more done and they are usually far more productive. This is not by accident but because they do not spend time or waste time complaining about negative things that they can change or resolve.

Positive people look at things in a positive manner and ask themselves "What can I do to fix this?" instead of "Why bother, this just plain sucks!" Positive people look for the good in things and then build on that part to change and remove the negative parts. The end result is that something negative has become something positive or, at the very least, something better or less negative.

Positive people are usually those people who are willing to dive in and tackle any situation with the belief that they can make it better or at least make a difference.

They are the people known for getting stuff done and not looking for excuses why something cannot be done. We all know the people who just complain yet do nothing to help make things better. We all work with them.

If you were a manager looking to hire someone for an important position, which type of person would you hire? Someone who would complain all the time but do nothing or someone who would take the bull by the horns and find a solution to almost any problem? Someone who has a "can do" attitude or someone with a "why bother" attitude? Someone who inspire others to do more and accomplish more or someone who joins in the complaint party and wastes time complaining instead of working towards a solution.

You have a choice as to which type of person you want to be. You can be a positive person and live a more productive and less stressful life or you can be a negative person and focus on just the worst in life. You can be the person people look up to and try to emulate or you can be the person people avoid. You can be the person that others think would do very well in a new position or the person who is rarely even considered.

It is your choice. Make the right one. And be positive.

Be Reliable

Generally speaking, everyone likes the people in their lives to be reliable and that includes the workplace as well. People who do what they say when they say it are people you can trust and rely on when it comes to getting things done and carrying their own weight.

Being able to work with someone on a project or task and knowing that they will have their part done on or before it is due can give an amazing amount of reassurance to a co-worker or manager. On the flip side, hoping against hope that someone will get his or her part done on time when they have a history of turning stuff in late if at all can induce stress and worry into the workplace.

If you are looking to establish yourself as a person who is worthy of continued and better employment then you need to establish yourself as someone that can be counted upon to do their part at all times without exception. You need to make people feel confident that you will do what you say when you say it without constant reminders or updates.

Being reliable is something that is very easy to do. All you have to do is a few simple things. A few of the most common and important parts of being reliable are:

Doing What You Say You Will Do

This is a simple one. If you say you are doing to do something or be somewhere, then just do it. Don't make excuses, don't blow stuff off and if for some reason something prevents you from doing something, give people advanced notice.

This is just all common sense and showing respect for others. While life is not perfect and sometimes things come up at the last minute, you can and should let other people know and you should also take this into consideration and never let things go until the last minute.

Your word should be your bond. People should feel that if you make a commitment that you will live up to it. They should feel that once something is left in your capable hands that they will not have to worry about it getting done.

Getting Work Done On Time

If something is due on a certain date, make sure you get it done by that date. Sometimes your tasks are combined with the work of other people and if one person's work is late or not done at all the entire project or process can be stopped dead in its tracks.

"Better late than never" is something that is not always true. Deadlines are put in place for a reason and that is to keep everything on track and organized.

This means managing your schedule and workload so that everything is done on or before the deadline or before you said you would have it completed by. It also means keeping others up to date on your progress, or lack of, so that they can plan the rest of the project accordingly.

In short, if you say you will have something done by a certain date and time, make every effort to see that you live up to that promise. All it takes is to miss one deadline or break one promise to cast everything else in the future in doubt.

Be On Time

I have friends and co-workers that I truly like but at the same time their ability to arrive for anything on time absolutely infuriates me. Some are so bad that we purposely tell them a dinner reservation is an hour earlier than it really is so they will be "on time"! While this does sound amusing, in the business world it can be a real problem.

Arriving on time for a meeting or appointment is not only the right thing to do it also shows respect for the other people at the meeting or appointment. You are letting them know that you value their time and schedule by arriving on time. If you constantly arrive late, you are telling them the exact opposite.

You are telling them that their time is of little concern to you and that other things were more important to you and this meeting.

Not a great message to send.

I always tell everyone I mentor or train that if you arrive at 9AM for a 9AM meeting, you are, in fact, late. I always recommend that people be where they are supposed to be 15-30 minutes early depending on the location of the appointment and the travel distance and weather. It is much better to sit in a coffee shop and have a cup of coffee for a while than it is to cut is so short you risk being late. If you are flying, try to get an earlier flight even though the next flight will get you to the meeting 3 minutes early. Stuff happens and it rarely happens at the best times!

If you are the host of the meeting, this is even more important as you are asking or demanding that others take time from their schedule to meet with you. I had a boss once who would hold webinars and he would NEVER start them on time. They were always 15-20 minutes late. During that time everyone had to stare at a wait screen on their monitor until he figured he would show up.

Now we realize that sometimes even the best efforts and precautions can result in lateness. There could be a massive traffic jam due to an accident or a plane could be delayed due to weather.

This happens and most people will understand this as long as you keep people informed. Call them or text them and make them aware of your updated arrival date.

This at least gives them the opportunity to use the time productively instead of just sitting there waiting.

In some cases you might just reschedule the meeting if the delays are severe. As I said, stuff happens and as long as it doesn't happen all the time and we keep others informed, we should be good.

Being on time just shows respect and concern for others. People who are always on time are more dependable and looked at more positively than their always late counterparts. If you want to be looked at in the best possible light, make an effort to always be on time.

Be a Self-Starter

I have worked with some very good people who produced some very high quality work over the years. Most of these people I would have recommended highly for a promotion or another job outside the company. But not all of them. Here's why:

Some of these people, though they did great work had to be told to do every little thing. Once they were told they did it and did it well but if no one told them to do something, it just didn't get done. Sometimes this caused delays or last minute frenzies to get something done that was needed right away.

If you told any one of these people to do A, B and C, they would do A, B and C. But if D, E and F also needed to be done, and they knew they had to be done and they had time to do them, they wouldn't do it until they were told. In other words, they lacked initiative and were not self-starts.

The problem with these worker was even though they did great work, they needed to be micro-managed to a large extent. They rarely did things on their own or took the initiative to do something more. They were willing to work, and work hard, but they never went out looking for things to do. Even when they were aware something had to be done unless they were told to do it nothing would get done.

The ability to work well without constant supervision and be counted on to do whatever it takes to get something done is a very admirable and important trait to have. Management loves this attitude because they do not have to constantly find things for you to do and can be relatively secure that if something needs to get done it will get done whether they point it out or not.

I am not saying to come in every morning and try and do everyone's work for them. But if you adopt an attitude of looking to see what else needs to be done after you have finished you work, it will be looked upon favorably by co-workers and everyone else.

There are many people out in the workforce that do good quality work. But combining good quality work with a can do attitude is something that is much more valuable in an employee. These are the people who get the recommendations and notices from their superiors. These are the people who are appreciated the most.

Reliability is something that is missing in a lot of people these days. They become so consumed with their own needs that they place themselves first and do not really care about anyone else. Sometimes this is done on purpose while other times it is done without thinking. Whatever the reason might be, it is an attitude that should be changed if you want to move ahead in your career.

If you do not think this is important, ask yourself how you would feel if the people who worked for you were not reliable and could not be counted on to do the right thing. How confident would you feel as an important deadline approaches? How much extra time would you have to spend to insure that everything is being done and everything will be ready on time?

Add that time to all the other time you need to do YOUR job and you will quickly see how have reliable and dependable people on your team is one of the most important things a manager or team pleader can have.

If you want to move up and ahead in your career, be as reliable and dependable as you can. It will help get you recognized, appreciated and rewarded for your efforts.

Be Confident But not Obnoxious

There are a lot of good and competent people in the workplace these days and if you want to get ahead, eventually you are going to compete with some of these people for a new or better job. Because of this, many times the best jobs or opportunities do not go to the most skilled or talented person but instead go to the person who APPEARS to be the best candidate.

Perception is important because when you interview with someone for a few minutes, or when you are talking to anyone that doesn't know you, all they have is what they feel about you after talking to you. So sometimes it is not what you say or how smart you are but instead how the other person perceives you to be.

One thing most people like in an employee is for that person to be confident in his or her abilities and capabilities. They want someone who is not afraid to take action and is not going to hesitate because they are unsure what to do next.

They want people who are going to act without fear and get the job done.

Confidence comes from your knowledge and experience. If you have an in-depth knowledge and a lot of experience in something, you are likely to be very confident in your abilities and not afraid to use them or make a decision when the time comes. This leads to increased productivity and being able to complete more tasks or work in any given amount of time.

Confidence also comes from how we were raised and our personal level of self-esteem. If we feel good about ourselves we are usually much more confident to make a decision or take action. But if we do not have a lot of self-esteem, or if we were raised to feel unworthy or inadequate, then sometimes we feel afraid or not capable of doing certain things. This can lead to several problems in the workplace.

On the other extreme, some people are so confident that they are downright obnoxious. While it is all right to feel you are the best at something it is NOT all right to constantly brag about it to others or act like you are somehow superior to everyone else. That kind of attitude is rarely received well and can limit your chances for advancement not to mention create very poor relationships with others.

We all know people like that who are constantly self-promoting and acting like they are so much better than everyone else. They are constantly talking about their achievements and at least some of the time exaggerating their skills or experience.

I am willing to bet that you know at least a few of these people in your life. Ask yourself how you feel about these people and I am sure you will understand why this attitude is not the best one to have in life.

The best approach to have in the workplace, and in most of the rest of your life as well, is that of someone who has confidence in what they do and are capable of but does not act superior or overbearing in front of others. In other words, it is perfectly fine to believe that you are the best but not OK to constantly tell everyone else. Be confident but not overtly so.

Being confident also means having a firm grip on your abilities so you know when to act and when to possibly seek advice or instruction on something. Confidence is not good when it tells you that you should do something that you are not skilled or trained in. While sometimes you might be forced to do such a thing in an emergency situation, doing things you do not know how to do rarely works out well.

So how do you become confident when you might not be all that confident today?

The first thing you should do is improve your education and skill sets so that you feel better and more confident in your abilities from a knowledge point of view. Then, you apply your knowledge in various situations and gain confidence in those abilities from actually applying them. The more you demonstrate your abilities the more confident you will become in those abilities.

Prepare yourself for what you expect to come down the road and show yourself that you can make the decisions when required and have success and success in your job. Over time you will show yourself that you can do what you need to do. As you gather more successes you will gain confidence. As you gain confidence you will be less afraid and more productive. It is a gradual process that will soon begin to steamroll.

As far as self-esteem is concerned, that is very important as well. If you have issues with self-esteem for any reason I strongly suggest you talk to someone or address those issues as quickly as possible. Issues with self-esteem can make advancing in your career and reaching your full potential a lot more difficult. Not impossible but a lot more difficult. If this is the case in your situation, speak to a therapist or counselor and begin to heal your problems and develop more self-esteem.

Ask for More Responsibility

Getting ahead in your career often means standing out from the rest of the workers and making sure that you get noticed. One very effective way of accomplishing this is to volunteer to do more work or get involved in more projects to increase your visibility within the company.

This is a little gesture that anyone can easily do but it can carry major benefits in getting your name and face recognized by those higher up in the company. Not only that but it also helps get you known as someone who is not afraid to step up and take on more responsibilities and assume a larger workload.

If you recall we had talked a bit about how important it is to be known as a problem solver and how managers and executives like people who solve problems and address situations before they ever reach the higher levels in the company.

Well, who better to accomplish that goal than the person they always see ready to step up and tackle something that might not even be in their area of expertise or job description?

We also already spoke about those people in the company who do a great job but don't ask for anything else or do anything else without being specifically asked. While these people might be very good at their job, they lack initiative and drive and this is something that is usually recognized by management. YOU want to set yourself apart from these people and show a stark contrast so that YOU are the one who is noticed and YOU are the one who is appreciated on a higher level.

The next time someone asks if there is someone who can take on a project or do a certain task, step up and volunteer. If the company needs someone to be part of a group or team to work on a project, request to be one of those people. The more you get involved in the more people you will be exposed to and the more people you will have the chance to impress. This is all about visibility and if you are as good as we hope you are, visibility is going to help you get to the next level in your career.

Volunteering is also a fairly risk free process as well as you usually get to see the task before hand and understand what is involved. So you can figure out if you have the time and skills necessary to do a good job and get the results people want or expect from the volunteer. After all, you do not want to volunteer for something you known little or nothing about and produce a bad or inferior result.

Exposure can work both ways and if you perform poorly the exposure you receive is not going to be good and can hurt your career instead of making it better.

Another consideration you might want to give is whether you have the time to take on this particular task in addition to your regular or normal workload. If you are so busy in your regular job that taking on more responsibility or more work is going to reduce the quality of your regular work, then it might be time to rethink volunteering. But be honest with yourself and do not use this as an excuse to keep you from volunteering at all.

When you do volunteer, make a good impression and make sure people are aware of your contributions. But do not do that in an obnoxious or obvious way. Do that by taking a position of visibility within the task or project. Take on one of the presenting roles or write the report that is part of the end of the task. Be one of the people who interviews others or take a leadership role in the project if available. You want to get involved in more things, meet and impress more people and get exposure to the decision makes in the company.

If the task or project takes you outside of the company that can be even better! Doing a presentation at a trade show or other external event can give your name a HUGE amount of exposure outside of your own company. There is no telling who might see you or where that appearance might take you.

That is also something that might look really well on your resume as experience. Especially if you are looking for a job at a company that was present at the event.

This is all about promoting yourself as someone who is not afraid to step up and help out. It is all about becoming known in a positive manner to as many people as possible. It is all about taking as many opportunities as you can to let others see how really good you are. Remember that your skills, accomplishments and work ethic are not doing you much good if no one is aware of them. So take every opportunity you can to showcase your skills, personality and the things that set you aside from everyone else.

Take Responsibility
for Your Actions

People who want to get somewhere in their career have to have integrity and the ability to take responsibility for their actions. While you sometimes see people lie, cheat and steal their way to the top, that rise is usually temporary and they soon plummet back down to reality in very short period of time.

We have all worked with people who never assumed responsibility for the things that they did unless, of course, the result was highly positive. When that occurred they were right up there, front and center, to accept the praise and rewards. But if things didn't go well, you had to search far and wide to find where they were hiding.

The reality of life and your career is that you are going to make mistakes. Hopefully not really big or career threatening mistakes but you are going to make mistakes. Everyone makes mistakes and no one is perfect. So we should not expect perfection only work towards it as best we can.

The key is what we do when we do make a mistake. Do you step up and acknowledge our mistake and take responsibility for it or do we make excuses and possibly even blame someone else for our mistake? What we do after the mistake is made is sometimes more important than the mistake itself.

I am a firm believer in honesty and integrity. I would love to see everyone be up front and honest with everyone else. Unfortunately that is not the case and we often need to deal with the fallout from other peoples actions. I believe that if you make the mistake you should step up and take responsibility for it. Hopefully you will have a solution to limit the problems caused by your mistake but even if you don't at least admit your mistake.

Assuming that you don't make mistakes very often your boss or management will likely understand and appreciate the fact that you stood up and took responsibility for it. Most managers like people with honesty and integrity and they look for that in their employees. I am not saying there won't be repercussions for admitting responsibility as there are also people looking for any excuse to take someone down or make them look bad in comparison. But most of the time, unless the mistake was really, really bad or was one of laziness or dishonest behavior, honesty is almost always the best policy.

Naturally, the best defense against making mistakes is to not make the mistake in the first place.

Watch what you are doing, be more careful and improve your knowledge to the point where you rarely have to guess or assume anything. If you are not sure ask questions until you are sure. But in those cases where you cannot be absolutely sure, make an informed decision and make sure you can back up or explain your actions should things go wrong.

There are two basic kinds of mistakes. There are avoidable mistakes and there are unavoidable mistakes. Avoidable mistakes are those mistakes we should have been able to avoid had we taken our time, prepared ourselves better, or not tried to take a shortcut to get something done faster or easier so we could go home early or leave for lunch on time. Another example of an avoidable mistake might be doing something that was against policy or procedure in order to make the task easier.

Avoidable mistakes are the ones that are the most difficult to explain and the mistakes you just have to "man up" (or "woman up") and just take responsibility for. Avoidable mistakes are the ones we have the most control over and the ones that we need to train ourselves to avoid through a great work ethic and a good skill set.

Unavoidable mistakes are those mistakes that come out of good intentions but something went wrong somewhere along the line. These can be very difficult to explain and sometimes mistakes just come about because something we thought was going to happen didn't.

For example, let's say we were creating an advertising flyer and we made the decision to use a certain picture and caption. You thought it looked great, everyone else thought it looked great and management signed off on it as well. No one had any other alternatives or suggestions. But you released it to the public and it bombed. Big time. People didn't respond to it and some people hated it. Sales tanked and the ad is pulled.

Now choosing that picture and wording turned out to be a mistake. Not a mistake due to laziness or cutting corners but a mistake none the less. But this was a mistake that no one saw coming. The ad wasn't offensive or inappropriate, people just didn't like it. Since we have no control over what people like or dislike, you can say this mistake was unavoidable.

In this case you would step up and take responsibility for the mistake and hopefully have some details as to what went wrong in the first place. Maybe you had a focus group that talked to customers to get their feelings or some other research. Whatever you had that helped explain things would be part of your explanation.

You see everyone makes mistake and while we should always look for ways to avoid mistakes we should always try and learn from them when they occur. When we take responsibility for something we usually stand a better chance of learning from that mistake so we don't do it again in the future. And when others can learn from those same mistakes, then everyone benefits.

So the next time something goes wrong and you had a part in the mistake, admit your part. Take responsibility for what you did and explain your reasons behind it. NEVER blame someone else as this will damage your integrity and reputation not only with management but with your co-workers as well. Just stand up, admit your role, and deal with the aftermath.

There have been several instances where mistakes have turned out to have silver linings. There have been times when people took responsibility only to have the silver lining make them come out looking pretty good in the process. But even if that doesn't occur, protect your reputation and integrity and do what many people seem to have a hard time doing.

Accept responsibility for your decisions and actions.

Do What Others Will Not Do

Sometimes the best things a person can do the get what they want out of life or their careers are the simplest things. This one in particular is so easy that most people never even think of it. Either that or they place themselves so above the other people this just slips by them.

If you want to get ahead, simply be willing to do the things that unsuccessful people are not willing to do. That means taking on the jobs that others refuse to do or simply ignore. It means not thinking that any task or action is beneath you or not worthy of your attention. This requires just a change in attitude and maybe a little reduction in your pride once in a while.

At one point or another we all started out pretty much at the bottom in our first job. For some of the lucky ones the bottom might not have been "rock bottom" but we considered it pretty much the bottom. In our position at the beginning we had to do pretty much what other people told us to do and usually that meant doing the real ugly or messy jobs. It usually meant burning the midnight oil while others went home on time as well.

Whatever those jobs might be, they certainly weren't the fancy, rewarding or high visibility jobs everyone was clamoring for. Instead they were the garbage jobs that had to be done but everyone hated doing. These jobs also pretty much flew under the radar as well, meaning those people who did them normally got little credit and no recognition. But they still needed to be done.

But sometimes doing those jobs does catch the attention of some other people and they might see your willingness to step in and help even though you might not be expected to normally do those jobs. Instead of turning them down or leaving them undone, you stepped in and took care of them so the project or others might move forward.

Other times you might gain knowledge or wisdom from doing those jobs as well. Nothing teaches someone something better than doing it first-hand. Simply doing something also creates a better awareness and sometimes helps change things for the better. In other cases you might learn something no one else knows and be able to use that knowledge in something else to improve the quality of your results.

This might mean taking on low value clients instead of the higher value ones. It might mean settling for lower sales from those clients as you build your clientele. Or, it might mean taking on a low volume client when everyone else is too busy for that small amount of business.

Whatever the reason might be, sometimes those small accounts might turn into huge accounts. Or one of those small accounts might recommend you personally to another, much larger, account because you took the time to help them.

The point I am trying to make is that sometimes things don't always look like what they really are. Throughout life we have many situation that are opportunities disguised as something much different. But those opportunities will only be discovered by those willing to sacrifice short-term for much more success further down the road. Don't think of the actual task but rather the potential benefits of performing it.

By doing things that other people either avoid or refuse to do you set yourself up to look like the ultimate team player willing to do anything in order to help the team. Since managers generally do not like prima donnas who feel that certain things are beneath them, showing the right attitude is bound to impress the people who count and open up doors for you somewhere down the road.

This is just one more thing you can do to elevate you from the rest of the pack. When you combine this with other strategies in this book it can make quite a difference in anyone's career.

Get Along with Others

Unless you are self-employed in a single person business, you will have people that you need to work with on a day to day basis. Even when you have a home office you still need to interact with people from the main office in order to do your job. Add to that vendors, subcontractors and customers and I do not think there is any job on the planet that anyone can do on their own without the need to interact with other people.

This is important because one of the characteristics of people who are in demand for all kinds of advanced and highly sought after jobs are good "soft skills". Soft skills are the skills we use to communicate with each other and handle all the day to day interaction between people. These skills are critical for anyone who wishes to get the most out of others as well as improving their own productivity.

Soft skills are basically skills that we use to understand how to treat other people and how to efficiently interact with them. Though not strictly limited to the following skills, these are the most common soft skills that most good people possess:

Dignity & Respect

This is something that should always be at the core of our beliefs and behavior. We should ALWAYS treat EVERYONE with dignity and respect regardless of how they might be treating us. We should always "take the high road" and not resort to retaliation or going down to a lower level because of how we are being treated.

There are several reasons for doing this. First, it is much harder to argue or confront someone who is nice and respectful to us in return. So treating people with dignity and respect will not only keep negative situations to a minimum, they will help keep them from escalating once they do occur. This enables people to remain more calm and communicate in a more productive and accurate manner.

Second, when you treat others right they tend to treat you in more of the same manner. They might not treat exactly like you are treating them but it almost will always be better than if you were nasty to them. After all, if you lie, steal or steal from people or take credit for their work or take other actions, the reaction from others will usually be swift and not very positive.

Listening Skills

Though most people do not think about this very much, everything in communication pretty much starts with listening. If you don't know how to listen effectively, you might never get the real message people are trying to deliver to you. No matter how well the other person speaks, if you don't know how to listen the entire communication process is doomed right from the start.

Communication Skills

How to communicate, meaning both speaking and listening is at the heart of everything we say and do throughout the day. Those who can communicate their thoughts, ideas and instructions generally get more done in less time and with less waste than poor communicators.

This is more than just speaking or listening. It also includes choosing the right words and delivering them so that they can be understood by everyone in the group. This often means speaking loudly enough and choosing the right setting so there are few distractions, if any, and where what is being said can be heard easily.

Public Speaking

Many of us can talk all day long to a co-worker or family and friends but when we are put in front of a large group of people, we totally freeze up.

This is normal for a lot of people but unfortunately as you move up in the company or take a higher profile position, talking to large groups is almost always part of the job. The last thing you want to have happen is that you lose out on a promotion because you cannot speak effectively to groups.

There are courses that you can take that will teach you effective techniques to reduce the fear and anxiety that sometimes accompanies speaking to groups. Or, you can gradually take more responsibility and speak to smaller groups at first to gain confidence and then gradually move up to larger groups. There is no one perfect method of addressing this fear as we are all different and find that different approaches work for different people.

I would suggest to anyone thinking about moving up in their career to check out a seminar or course on public speaking. They are given at colleges and Universities all over as well as in Adult Education as well. Public Speaking knowledge will help you in speaking engagements as well as in interviews when you are seeking a promotion or a better job outside the company. It is almost always better to get these skills before you have to have them so you will have a chance to practice them and become comfortable.

Conflict Resolution

Conflict resolution skills are very important to possess because they teach you how to resolve issues and situations as they occur with a minimum of trouble and lost time.

No matter how well people get along and how perfect the office environment is there are always going to be problems. Without the skills to address these problems and issues when they arise we run the risk of having even small issues turn into massive problems.

Conflict resolution skills give you the ability to resolve problems in the right way by identifying the root cause of the problem (which is not always obvious or what you might think it is!) and to craft a solution that makes everyone happy. These skills can save a company a LOT of time and money is used properly.

Recovery Skills

Sometimes when problems occur it is how we act after the problem that can make all the difference in the world. There are examples of customers experiencing problems but then are so impressed by how the business handled those problems that they became customers for life! While I certainly do not endorse creating problems so you can be the hero and impress the customer, these skills are very handy to have when you need them.

Telephone Skills

I cannot begin to tell you how many people I know that are very good at their jobs and very intelligent yet they no idea how to use the telephone properly and effectively.

The telephone can be your greatest asset or your greatest liability depending on how you go about using it.

In some cases the only time you might interact with a remote employee or a customer might be over the phone. Knowing how to use the phone properly can help improve the relationship between both people while also lowering the stress involved in any given situation.

You can also use proper telephone practices to cut down on time wasting activities such as "phone tag" while also helping make your business phone system more customer friendly and efficient. While none of these things might seem like huge issues to you, they can represent significant issues with other people and your customers. It just makes sense to do the things you need to do to make using the phone in your business easier and less stressful for everyone concerned.

Cultural Differences

Today with so much business being done digitally and the increased ethnic diversity throughout the world we are finding ourselves interacting with many more cultures and ethnic groups than we did just a few decades ago. Each of these groups have their own customs and differences and if we want to interact effectively with them we must develop a knowledge of these people so we can choose our words and phrases appropriately.

The last thing we want to do is innocently use a word or phrase that might be insulting or demeaning to another person. When this happens we have to go into recovery or damage control mode and this can cost us valuable time and resources. It is much better to understand things up front and choose our approach and wording then than just to hope what we do is all right and "wing it". As with a lot of other things in life, understanding something in the beginning and taking precautions before a problem is created is by far the best way to go.

Anger Management

Life in general can be a very stressful process that sometimes pushes us to our limits or beyond. This can also happen to those around us and sometimes we bear the brunt of their stress and frustration. Because of this, learning effective ways or controlling our anger or other emotions can help us remain in control and productive in the face of adversity.

We often hear of things like road rage and people "losing it" and starting fights and altercations in public and in the workplace. This happens when people are no longer capable of controlling how they feel and how they react to their environment.

Anger management not only allows us to function on a more emotionally stable manner but also allows us to help other do the same and to help control negative situations so that everyone is able to behave rationally and safely.

This is not a skill we usually think about but still a skill that is very useful in both the workplace and at home.

All of these skills have one thing in common. They all allow us to work together and interact with each other in a better and more efficient and enjoyable manner. When it comes to your career and getting along with the people you work for, these skills can help you get a reputation as someone who easily gets along with others and is widely respected.

This in turn will result in people talking about you in more favorable terms and further enhancing your reputation and image with others in the company. Then, when an opportunity comes up that you are interested in, there will be a lot of good-will and positive comments about you that will make you stand out from the rest of the applicants.

One past thing to consider is that a management position, even at the lowest levels, requires a high degree or interaction with other people. Because of this, people being considered for these positions must have a reputation for being able to get along with other people and lead everyone. You cannot lead a group effectively if they do not respect you. Few people realize this but now you do.

So make every effort to get along with other people and demonstrate this as often as you possibly can.

Believe me when I say that people will notice and that you will benefit from doing this the next time you are being considered for a promotion or other position. This is just one more thing you can add to everything else to make you look more and more like the perfect candidate.

Participate

Here is a quick hitter as we have already touched on this subject when we talked about volunteering and asking for additional work or responsibilities. But participating is more than just doing more and asking for more responsibility. Participating means getting more involved in the company or office work environment.

While some people tend to stay by themselves and not get involved in the office environment, doing so is usually regarded as sort of an isolationist behavior. That means keeping to yourself and not being "one of the guy or girls". That can cause others to look at you as an outsider or someone who think they are better than everyone else.

While you don't have to let co-workers into your inner circle of friends or go out with them after work or in social settings, you should be friendly and participate in office conversations, parties, discussion and other activities. You should also participate in company activities and events as well.

That means going to the company picnic or to company sponsored events. You don't need to stay the entire time and sometimes it is often OK to just make an appearance. The idea is to get involved so people see another side of you other than the person who just sits at their desk and works all day.

Being involved also allows other people to get to know you better and become more aware of the type of person you really are. This can help others see you in a higher or better job within the company. You would be surprised who you might have access to at these functions that you might otherwise never really see. I'm not saying that you should use these events as networking sessions or anything like that but you can always introduce yourself to people you want to meet so they know you exist.

As far as participating in office events or social groups there are a couple of things you should be aware of that might cause you a problem or two. I would stay clear of groups that constantly gossip or otherwise participate in negative behavior directed at either the company or groups or individuals. You do not want to develop a reputation as someone who gossips or talks behind the backs of other people.

You also do not want to get involved with people that are not exhibiting your work ethic or values either. I am not saying to think that you are better than anyone else just to be careful who you associate with.

This is because, like the gossiping example above, you can frequently be thought of as guilty by association.

For example, if you associate with people that are known to be anti-company or are known to take credit for things they didn't do or similar behavior, other people might feel that you are also doing the same thing because you hang out with the people that do. While this might not be fair it is a perception that can do you and your career a lot of harm if the right people hear the wrong things about you.

But if you can participate on a group level with other people in the office and try to fit in and be "one of the guys" you will usually find out that you will be better received and respected. You will not be thought of as a snob or someone who feels they are better or superior in any way.

Just try your best to participate in office and company activities and let people get to know you. This is one tool at your disposal that can actually be fun to use yet provide you with a lot of benefit and exposure. But do it for the right reasons. If people get the impression that you are doing this just to promote yourself and rise in the company they will react very negatively very quickly.

Just become engaged in your work environment, be careful and do it for the right reasons and you will be fine.

Create a Powerful Resume

Up to this point we have discussed several things you can do to make yourself thought of as a better candidate for a new or better job. Up until now we have focused on how to make it difficult NOT to hire you. Now we are going to switch gears for a moment and discuss how to start preparing yourself for the next opportunity that might come your way.

As far as opportunities are concerned, many of them do not announce themselves. They just appear, seemingly out of nowhere, when you least expect them and are often unprepared for them. To make sure that you do not find yourself unable to take advantage of an opportunity when it does arrive, we are going to talk about one of the most important things any job applicant needs to do.

That is creating the very best and most compelling resume.

Your resume very often is your introduction to the person responsible for at least starting the hiring or evaluation process. If your resume is not compelling, if it does not stand out from the others and if it does not reflect every single advantage and qualification you possess, you might never go any further in the process.

So designing or updating your resume should be carefully done and not done in 4 minutes the night before you need to apply for a new job. You should have a resume ready and waiting for whenever you might need it. You might have to tweak it a bit or add a last minute item or two but the resume should be carefully created and be there waiting for you whenever you need it.

Two Main Types of Resumes

There are two primary types of resumes. There are targeted resumes which we would use for a specific job or type of job and there are generic resumes which would be used for any job you might want to apply for.

Generic resumes are generally thought to be the weaker of the two type because they are generalized views of who you are and what you bring to the table. They are not specific and sometimes they leave a lot of information about you off the resume. Generic resumes do not portray you in the best manner for certain jobs.

Targeted resumes are resumes that are put together to address a specific position or opportunity.

Every entry and word choice is designed to make you appear to be the strongest candidate for that particular job. You would enter the experience and qualifications that are strongest for that job and that job only on your targeted resume. This helps make your skills and experience stand out from the very beginning. Because of this targeted resumes are the most impressive and have the biggest effect on interviewers and screeners.

It is my opinion, and this opinion is shared by most people, that we only use generic resumes when we are trying to introduce ourselves to a new company for an unknown job. While this usually doesn't happen all that often, a generic resume MIGHT be OK in that context. But for all other uses or applications, a targeted resume is the best way to go.

I even take this a step further and design several resumes each targeted to a specific job or opportunity. These resumes are very similar but each one is optimized for a specific job or opportunity. Some entries are slightly changed, the opening statement might be slightly different and you can pick and choose specific experience and education to showcase your skills more accurately.

Today with computers it is extremely easy to create a very targeted and unique resume for any job.

Once you have the main outline and resume created, you just save the template and then create as many targeted resumes as you need by changing a few items and wording. Once you have done a couple you should be able to comes up with a professional looking and reading very targeted resume in less than 30 minutes!

What Your Resume Needs to Do

Your resume should be considered as your introduction. Instead of you being able to shake someone's hand and engage them in conversation, your resume is how you are going to be evaluated by people involved in the evaluation and hiring process.

You also need to be aware of one very sobering fact. Resumes are usually gathered as they appear and then are looked at by someone after many resumes have been received. Depending on the particular job and how it has been advertised, there could be a dozen or several hundred resumes for that person to look at.

This means that the person who looks at your resumes is not going to have time to read the great American novel of a multi-page diatribe on how great you are and why you are perfect for the job. Instead, he or she is likely to just read the first couple of sentences and skim over the rest to see if anything catches their eye. They are not going to stop and read the entire resume. At least not at this point.

After scanning the resumes and reducing them to just a few, the person is then more likely to go through each resume in more detail and from those resumes select the people who will be invited in for a face to face or phone interview. But if your resume does not make it into this final group you have no shot at getting an interview.

Because of this, your resume MUST capture the interest of the person who is reading it. It MUST make them feel that they HAVE to or WANT to read more. That is the only way you have a prayer of making it further into the process. If the person reading your resume is bored, or if they do not see anything special, your resume is likely heading for the shredder.

This is why a targeted resume is so much better. You can custom design your objective header and resume to showcase the best and most relevant parts of your education and experience and help the evaluator clearly understand why you deserve more consideration. The purpose of your resume is to get you in for an interview. If it doesn't accomplish that, nothing else you do will help you land that job!

Your Cover Letter

Your cover letter is basically an introduction to your resume although some people might skip over your cover letter and go straight to your resume.

But your cover letter is where you get to show a little bit more of yourself personally through your writing and give them some more insight into who you are, why you are a great fit for the job and why they should want to find out more about you.

Since we can never be sure which is going to be read first, the cover letter must be specific and compelling enough so that the person reading it become interested in looking into you more. It MUST make them want to read your resume in detail. We accomplish this by having targeted cover letters as well.

Sending out the same cover letter to every job you apply for is one sure way of getting both the cover letter and resume tossed into the reject pile. Trust me when I say that most of the people who evaluate candidates know a generic document when they see it. Their reaction is usually that if a candidate did not think the position was important enough to send a customized resume and/or cover letter in when they were applying then the interest wasn't really there.

Another reason for not using a generic cover letter is that companies do not want to waste their time interviewing people who apply to every job that is posted whether they really want it or not. The process of sending out 500 resumes to see what interest there is out in the market is not an effect way to get a job you really want.

Make your cover letter as specific as possible and give them all the reasons you can give them as to why you want the job and why you are the perfect candidate for it.

Don't be shy but don't be obnoxious either. You want to be seen as sincere and truthful in both the resume and cover letter.

Your cover letter should also have you contact information in it so that if your resume should get lost by mistake the cover letter will still allow the company to get in touch with you should they want to learn more about you.

How Long Should a Cover Letter or Resume Be?

Your cover letter should be no longer than one page and the font used should be easy to read. Personally I prefer fonts no smaller than 12 for letters or resumes. Keep in mind that if the font is too small and the person reading it has to struggle, they are more likely to just toss it aside and move on to the next applicant.

As far as resumes are concerned, one page is preferable but two pages is OK if there is sufficient content to fill the two pages. Keep in mind the person reading these documents doesn't have a lot of time to go through everything so they will not read through a 5 page resume to see if you are what they are looking for.

What Should I Include?

As you may or may not have realized by now, we have limited space available on both the cover letter and resume.

So we should choose our content carefully so it provides the most impact within that short amount of space. In other words, if it isn't going to help us land the job or enable someone to get in touch with us, it shouldn't be included!

By all means include your education and any relevant or impressive experience you might have. As far as education is concerned include you primary education such as college degrees and such but leave off non relevant courses or programs unless you need them to fill space. Again, every line on that resumes should speak directly to the job you are applying for.

When it comes to experience, list relevant experience but make sure you do not show any gaps in employment which might raise a red flag with some people. List the aspects or responsibilities of each job as they directly pertain to the job you are applying for. You want to draw specific connections between what you are doing now or have done in the past and what is required for the job you are applying for now.

Speaking of drawing connections, both our resumes and cover letters should make it as easy as possible to see valid and direct connections between us and the job we are applying for. Do not hope or expect that the person will see these connections. Put them right in front of their eyes so they definitely make those connections and draw the same conclusions. Even if they already see the connections and realize the value, seeing them in print will make you seem more impressive and a better overall fit.

If you are an experienced candidate, only place you most impressive experience and qualification I the resume to keep it within the one or two page limit. After all, you want to show you very best and the other stuff will not help you nearly as much as you most impressive items.

But if you are a first time job hunter or a young person with limited experience then look for ways to make yourself appear better in the reader's eyes. Include things that show drive or initiative like things you joined or volunteered with. Then, as your career gets longer and you've accomplished more, you can remove some of the earlier items and replace those with more impressive qualifications and experience.

Your Choice of Words

Sometimes the way you explain something or the words you use can significantly increase the value of what you have accomplished. For example, you can write down on your resume "created paychecks for 15 employees" or you could write "was responsible for payroll activities and management for field service staff". Both say the same thing but one sounds more impressive than the other.

When it comes to what you say and how you say it, you need to understand that this is a competition. People are always looking for ways to get to that interview and make themselves look better than the other applicants.

You need to do the same. You need to make yourself look like the PERFECT person for the job. Not one of the best but THE BEST! Everyone else is doing this and if you decide to be modest and hold back, someone else is likely to walk off with the job!

That being said, do not lie on your resume. If you have never done something, do not say that you did. If you don't have the required education or experience, don't put down that you did. Not only do people check up on these things before hiring, they can also check after hiring and any lies or false statements could result in your immediate termination!

So be honest but make yourself out to be the very best you can be. Because everyone else is doing the same things. It is up to you to do them better and make yourself one of those people heading into that all important face to face interview.

Ace that Interview

Interviews are where you get to show other people what it is about you that makes you special and the best choice for this position. It is where you get to expand on what was in your resume and to answer questions designed to bring out your real experience and skills sets. In other words, this is where you get to sell yourself to others.

While that might sound a bit crass, it is an accurate description of what you really are doing in an interview. You are the product that you are trying to convince the other people or company to "buy". Your experience and skills sets are your "product features" and during the interview you are going to try and match your features with what the company needs. When all is said and done if your "product" is the best product for their needs, you will get the job!

Before we get started, one little bit of advice for you: Sometimes it is helpful for you to create a sheet outlining more of your experience and qualifications that you want people to be aware of.

While this is too much information to place in a cover letter or a resume, you can bring this to the interview and leave a copy of it with the interviewer. They can then refer back to it later and your resume might then have more information attached to it than anyone else's. Since you might be interviewing with more than one person, bring several copies of these "fact sheets" with you to the interview.

Now, on with the interview:

Throughout the interview you will be asked a series of questions designed to give the prospective employer an idea of who you really are and whether you have the skills and abilities necessary to do the job. They will ask about your education and experience as well as what you are currently doing. These are the easy questions and your answers should be truthful and honest while at the same time be crafted to show yourself in the best possible light.

There will also be other questions designed to see what type of person you are in terms of work ethic, how you relate to others as well as your values, morals and other personal characteristics. Some of these questions will be open and straight forward while others might be disguised to get you to say things you might not want to say. So you need to be careful.

For example, do not complain about past jobs. If they ask you if there were things you didn't like about past employment or why you want to leave you current job, do not tell them your boss is a jerk or the company is lousy to work for or anything like that.

This shows poor character and a possible problem with getting along with others. Interviewers like positive responses so give them positive responses.

For example, you might say that your current job does not challenge you enough and that you are looking to learn new things, improve your skills and challenge yourself in your career. You might tell them how you heard wonderful things about their company and that you can see a long-term future with them. In other words, tell them positive things about why you want the job. Leave the negative stuff unsaid.

You should also research the company before the interview as well. Learn as much about them as possible so you can use that information in your answers as well. This shows the interviewer that you can serious about this position because you took the time to learn about the company.

Every answer to every question should be designed to make you look your best and enhance your appeal to the interviewers. Any answer that is negative or even neutral should be redesigned to make you look better. Even negative aspects of your career or gaps in your qualifications should be "massaged" to make them seem less negative than they might really be.

Think about the entire interview as a process that starts with you in the middle of a line. On the right side of the line is getting the job and on the left side of the line is being disqualified from the process.

Every question you answer and every statement you make should have the result of moving you closer to the right side of that line or closer to being offered the job. This way of looking at things is important because it allow you to see that for every wrong or negative answer you actually have to "make up" ground just to get back to where you once were. So take each question seriously and answer it so that you look your best.

Every question the interviewer askes you, even the seemingly innocent ones, are designed to get some more knowledge from you about who you really are. Don't let your guard down and fall into a false sense of security. Answer every question only after thinking about what it is you should be saying.

Interview Do's

Do prepare for the interview. Read a book on interviews so you know what to expect. It might even be a good idea to go on a couple of interview just to get some experience before the really important ones.

Do answer every question in such a way that you look like the perfect person for the job.

Do connect the dots for the interviewer so they see direct and relevant connections between you and your experience.

Do show up on time and wear appropriate clothing. For women a tasteful dress or outfit and for men, a suit or jacket and tie. Do this regardless of the type of job you are applying for. It shows you are committed and serious about the opportunity.

Do take the interview seriously. Answer every question carefully.

Do ask questions if there is something you want them to know about you. Asking a question to draw out the response you want to make can be an effective way of getting your most important points across.

Do have a personality. Relax and don't be stiff and too serious. Don't make jokes but you can be cheerful.

Do show some passion. Let them know you are passionate about this job. Share with them your thoughts about the job and how you can make a difference. Make it seem like more than just a paycheck for you. Show them that you care.

Do thank them for their time even if you didn't think the interview went well.

Interview Don'ts

Don't be late. This shows disregard and disrespect for those who were taking the time to meet with you. If you cannot be on time because of traffic or some other reason, call and let them know so they can either reschedule or know when you are going to arrive.

Don't be smug. Even if you are the very best person for the job, don't make them feel that you are doing them a favor by considering to work for them.

Don't speak before you think. Innocent questions can have some pretty important reasons behind them

Don't be in a rush. Give them the time they need to ask their questions. You do not want to make them feel that there are more important things in your life other than this interview. Even if they are late, don't rush.

Don't lie or make false statements or claim things that aren't true. Even if you land the job you place your continued employment at risk.

After the Interview

It is likely that you are just one of several people that were called in for a first or possibly second interview. Hopefully you made a good impression and were thought of favorably. But sometimes when several people are interviewed by the same person for the same job, details get blurred and people get confused with one another.

Also, sometimes after the interview is over we realize that we forgot to mention something important or wanted to bring other information up in the conversation but never got the chance.

If either of these situations pertains to you and your interview then this one last piece of the puzzle might be very worthwhile for you. Even if this isn't the case for you, doing this anyway will give you an added chance to set yourself apart from everyone else.

After every interview, as soon as you can send a follow-up letter, or e-mail if you have the person's e-mail address, to the person or people you talked to thanking them for their time and letting them know you enjoyed the interview.

You can also tell them how great a fit you think you are for the position and even use this opportunity to once again draw some pretty specific parallels between the job requirements and your specific skills and experience. This is also a perfect opportunity to add additional information you want people to know.

We should say at this point that this is just a very high level overview of the interview process and there are many more things you might need to be aware of. We suggest you read a book on interview tactics and questions to better prepare yourself. If you are considering going for a very high level position where there is a lot at stake, then you might even want to hire a coach to help guide you through the process. It make be money very well spent.

Advance Properly

Though there might be some disagreement when it coming to how to advance I your career, I have just one small bit of advice. Advance ethically and honestly through the ranks. Do not step over people or take advantage of others in the process. This can often do you more harm than good in your career.

We all know people who always seem to do anything and everything to get ahead. They schmooze the boss, they do personal favors for management and overall are just your average "brown nose". There is no doubt that this sometimes works but in most case it also has consequences that can prevent you from doing your best moving forward.

I still say to those people will do anything and everything that advancing through the ranks based on skills and performance is the best way to go. Not only will you earn and deserve every promotion or new job but you will do so by keeping your integrity and reputation intact.

There also will be far fewer people talking behind your back or even sabotaging your efforts because you took advantage of them on the way up.

Your ethics and integrity take years to build and establish but they can be torn down in a matter of minutes by making the wrong choices or doing the wrong things. I have seen many a meteoric rise followed by an even faster free fall because the person had no support on the way up or even more important, on the way down.

Though this approach might keep you from rising as fast as you would like and while these so-called "shortcuts" might seem extremely appealing, I advise you to resist the temptation and build your career on solid knowledge, exemplary performance and solid foundation of ethics and values.

While this does not mean that you should be a doormat for anyone else or let anyone take advantage of you, it does mean that you should take the high road and act only in ways that you would like other people to act in relation to you and your job. It is only fair to everyone.

Promote Yourself

We have already said several times that getting a new job or moving ahead in your career is very much a competition. After all it makes sense that if something is valuable and desirable to you it probably makes other people feel the same way. All of that means that it is going to be up to you to portray yourself in the best light so that you look like the perfect candidate for the job or opportunity.

I want to share something with you that you might already know but possibly do not. It might sound a bit conceited or obnoxious depending on your point of view but regardless of how you might feel about it, you cannot deny the truth behind it.

If you achieve something in your career but no one knows about it, other than personal pride, it will do you little good.

If you do something above and beyond but no one is aware of it, you will likely see little benefit from doing it.

If you possess a skill set but no one is aware that you possess it, you cannot use that skill set to its full potential.

If you do great work but don't take credit for it or allow other to take credit for work you have done, that work will not benefit you.

In other words, if you do something good in your job but no one knows about it, the benefit for doing whatever that was is going to be minimized. In order for you to become known for your successes and capabilities, your actions are always going to have to be accompanied by a little bit of self-promotion.

The thought of promoting yourself is objectionable to some people because they envision someone taking credit for everything they do and generally being a credit-taking jerk always looking to tell everyone how good they are and brag about 3everything they do.

But I am not saying you should do that or even recommend you do that. What I want you to do is make sure people know what you have done in a roundabout and under the radar manner. In other words, promote yourself quietly and ethically without being obnoxious about it.

For example, if you routinely come in early or stay late and your boss is in his office, stop by and give him a "hello!" or a ""Working late to?" kind of greeting to make sure he is aware of your presence outside of normal hours.

Don't do this every single time or be obvious about it. Just do little things to make sure he or she knows you are there. It might even mean just dropping off something or asking them a question on what you are working on.

If you are working on a project, request a more visible role such as a presenter or other visible role so that people are aware of your contribution. Don't do the lion's share of the work and let everyone else, or someone else, take all the credit.

There are ways to make sure people are aware of what you are doing to benefit the company or to see that projects are done correctly and on time. But remember if no one is aware of these special things they will never be an advantage to you. Granted there will be time when you want to do something nice for someone without claiming recognition or credit but that should be your choice and no one else's.

Get Published!

One common problem a lot of job applicant's face is that they have limited credibility outside their own company. By that we mean that no one really knows them except for personal friends or associates that might also have relationships with other companies. But if there are no personal recommendations then all someone has to go by is a resume and cover letter and we all know that is not necessarily an accurate representation of who an applicant really is.

We talked already about the need to become an authority or a "go to" person and the benefits of developing a reputation as someone who gets things done and is not afraid to work hard to get the right results. But again, sometimes that reputation exists only within the company you work for and not anywhere else. So what we need is a way to establish our credentials and create name awareness outside our company.

One very effective way to accomplish this is to have an article or paper published in a trade or industry publication. You might write an article on a new process or procedure or how you made improvements on something that wound up saving the company time and / or money. Once this article is published along with your name, you will get publicity and exposure outside your own company and within it at the same time.

There are many ways to get your name published. As we mentioned you can write articles for a magazine or even an industry blog or website. You can do this over time and create a following both in magazines and online as well. The more items you get published and the more your name is seen in print, the more credibility you will establish.

You might even write a book like this one and self-publish it and then use that book as a reference in your resume or other publication. An applicant that has written 5 books on a subject will almost always look better on paper than someone who hasn't. It doesn't matter if anyone has actually purchased or read them, only that you actually wrote them. Having a book with your name on the cover enhances your overall value and reputation. It might be just enough to get you in for that first interview or have your name picked over someone else.

Check out your trade publications and see how you can go about getting an article published. See if there are blogs you can post to as well.

The funny thing about getting your name in print is that some people might not remember where they saw it but seeing your name on a resume might make you should more familiar if they had seen your name in print as well.

Like anything else though, make sure your name is found only on good quality and high value content. Seeing your name on that kind of material is a good thing. Seeing your name attached to poor writing or garbage content is not a good thing. So always go for quality over quantity.

Another option for you might be to start your own blog if your career is something that is usually seen in blog format. You can easily host your own blog for less than $20 a year and it can be your own forum for your thoughts, training and the exchange of information and opinions. Not only can this give your reputation and credibility a significant boost but you might also find that you can earn some decent money from your blog as well. But for now, just contrite on getting your name out there for everyone to see.

Network

In many ways a lot has changed over the year when it comes to advancing your career and going after bigger and better jobs. The Internet is giving us access to job postings all over the country and even the world and these make you aware of opportunities that you might otherwise never knew existed. But even though many things are constantly changing, something always seem to remain the same and we must be aware of those things and use them to our advantage.

What has not changed is that most mid-level and higher jobs are not filled strictly by online job posting sites, newspaper advertisements or anything like that. These jobs are filled through personal recommendations or references from others. That means someone who is well known and respected by a company recommends or vouches for someone who is interested in the job. These personal recommendations carry a LOT of weight for several reasons.

First, no interviewer really knows the people that they are interviewing. We all put on our best face and attitude and we "color" all our statements and comments with one thing in mind and that is to get the job. The result is that even though these interviewers are often very experienced, there is always at least a little guesswork involved in the process. Having a personal recommendation from someone you trust removes at least some of that guesswork.

Second, with a personal recommendation, the thought is that people are not going to recommend a bad candidate because it would ultimately reflect poorly upon them as well. So they will recommend only strong candidates in the hope of strengthening their relationship in the future. Since the thought is that these people see the applicants as they really are and not what they want others to see, they will get a more accurate feel for the person than the interviewer.

Third, a personal recommendation can often cut through a lot of the process and even eliminate the need to post or advertise the position. This not only saves time and money, it helps the company discover highly qualified people in less time and with greater accuracy.

Fourth, and few people rarely think of this, whenever a company hires anyone, they have to invest a lot of time and money into training that person to do things the way the company wants things done and to learn their computer systems and procedures.

This can take weeks or months and if by the time this training is finished they discover the applicant was not who they thought they were, all of that time and money has been wasted.

By getting personal recommendations from trusted individuals, they can make much more accurate determinations and trust the evaluations provided by these people. That means more accurate hires and much less wasted time. It is just much smarter and cost efficient to hire the right person the first time.

Now that we all understand the value of a personal recommendation, we need to take the next step and figure out how to get more and more of those personal recommendations coming in on our behalf. That means making ourselves known to as many people as possible and developing relationships with those people.

Networking can take place in many different ways. Here are just a few of the most common ways people network:

Join Industry Associations

If your business or industry has a trade organization or professional organization, join it and get involved with the activities. People from all over the country will take part in these events and it can bring a wealth of contacts into your network.

Join Local Civic Groups

Local civic groups and other local organizations can place you with leaders and people of influence within the local community. These are the people who know what is going on in the area and this can prove valuable if you are looking to stay in the area throughout your career.

Trade Shows

Trade shows will give you exposure to a lot of different people from all kinds of companies. If you can arrange to work a booth at one of these shows you can get exposure to a wide number of people in a very short period of time.

Local Volunteering

Volunteering your skills and services is a great way to get exposure while doing some good deeds along the way. Working side by side with other people is a great way of getting people to know who you are and what you are all about. Volunteering is also a commendable trait and one that is often thought very highly of by most people.

Sponsorships

Sponsorships mean supporting local groups or events in your area either through the donation of products and services or assisting in staffing the event in exchange for promotional credit and exposure. If you company gets exposure that can lead to you capitalizing on their good name as well.

Business Groups

Local business groups can put you in contact with the decision makers in your area. These are the people who can make stuff happen for you if given the chance. Being able to work with them on projects and events will allow you to help them while demonstrating and showcasing your skills at the same time. This can leave a powerful impression on some influential people.

Networking Do's:

Do get your name and face out to as many people as you can.

Do try and create long-term relationships with other in your groups.

Do make this about helping and getting involved and NOT about personal promotion. People will see through that really quick and will not think highly of you if they realize that is why you are there.

Do volunteer for things to make your presence known and appreciated.

Do learn about others and how to help them while showcasing your skills and abilities.

Do take advantage of opportunities to help other whenever you can.

Do help the organization if you do join one. That is your primary purpose.

Networking Don'ts:

Don't make this all about you. You are there to help others not promote yourself.

Do not start off by promotion yourself or asking for favors or recommendations.

Do not be aggressive. It takes time for people to get to know the real you and become comfortable with you.

It is very hard to get access to some jobs because of the power of a personal recommendation. Networking will not only help make you aware of opportunities before they are known to everyone else but they will also give you a chance to use a personal recommendation to help pave the way for you.

Remember that there has to be a balance between what you give to others and what you hope to receive in return. Do not make it obvious as to why you are there. If you are there to promote yourself, do so but be discreet and do not start right away. Do some good for others before trying to do some good for yourself.

Act Like a Consultant

Someone told me to do this years ago and I never really understood what he was trying to teach me until years later. But instead of looking at your job or career as an employee, look at it from the viewpoint of a consultant. Consultants are people who come in with the intent of making something better or performing a certain function. These are exactly the same things employees should be doing as well. So why not develop the same attitude as a consultant?

Think about that for a moment. Consultants are brought in to make things better and to solve problem no one else in the company is capable of solving. They come in a look at everything from their own perspective and look for anything that might be wrong and decide how to make it better. They don't take anything for granted, they don't let anything stand in their way. They are results oriented and they will do whatever is necessary to make things run better and more efficiently.

Now, doesn't that sound like an ideal employee attitude?

Don't you think a company would want someone who would work tirelessly to get the best results and do what was necessary to achieve them?

Don't you think a company would want someone to look at things from another perspective and spot things that could be made better, more efficient and more productive?

Don't you think a company would appreciate someone who could get things done without constant supervision and take a proactive look at how business is being done?

The answer to all of these questions would definitely be "YES!" unless there were other agendas and factors in play. But most companies would love to have a staff that was committed to making things better and would not be afraid to take action to get the results they were looking for.

How many times have you heard someone say that something "was not my problem"? Or say that a certain task was someone else's job and not theirs? These are the attitudes that help keep things the same whether they are good or bad for the company. What companies need to day are employees that are not afraid to work hard and are willing to get the job done.

But you can be that employee if you are not that employee already. YOU can be the one who take the initiative to make things better and more efficient.

You can be the one who thinks like a consultant and looks at things from a different angle and notices things others do not care enough to notice. You can become the one people look to for a fresh or new perspective.

This does not take a lot of effort. It only takes a bit of commitment, a change in attitude and a bit of finesse when people might take issue or resent what you are trying to do. But the advantages and benefits of adopting this kind of attitude can be substantial to someone looking to advance within the company. Not only will you be looked at as a problem solver, you will be recognized as someone with drive and initiative. That is something many people seem to lack these days.

Consultants are driven by results and independent thinking. That is something valued by most companies as well as most managers. This is something we are all capable of doing once we assume responsibility for our actions and leave some old misconceptions behind. In other words, we need to take the initiative instead of waiting for someone else to do what we were capable of doing all along.

Remember that we make our own luck in life and our career through doing the tough jobs, taking the initiative and doing the right thing. Being willing to do those things will place us in the top tier of most workforces and make us great candidates for advancement and promotions down the road.

Always Try for the Win-Win Outcome

Back when I was very young, I did odd jobs like mowing lawns and trimming bushes to get money to do the things that I enjoyed as a kid. One particular job was a fairly large job that would give me a few weeks spending money so I really wanted the job. I gave a pretty low price and the homeowner told me I could have the job but we would pay me more because my price was too low.

I learned a huge listen from that experience. One that was worth far more than the money I earned from that job!

I realized as I did the job that I wanted to do a much better job because of the way the homeowner treated me. I actually did even more work than we agreed upon and I took extra time and care to make sure everything looked not just good, but perfect. The homeowner loved the results and I got a lot more work and referrals from him during the next few years.

I learned from that experience that when you treat people right and when you look to get them as much of what they need, while still taking care of your own needs, that they will appreciate you more and you will benefit from that attitude far after the job is done. It is something I have experienced over and over again throughout my career.

I have had people work for me and do things they told me they wouldn't do for anyone else. Not because I was a really special person or anything like that but because I treated them well and respected their time and their lives. In other words, I looked out for them as well as my interests.

Today it seems that we have moved away from that approach to business and the "winner take all" or the "cutthroat" model of business has taken over. You know the feeling. The hardball approach to get the best price or the most from the customer or the manager trying to get the last drop of work out of an already tired and stressed out employee. You might succeed in your efforts but you have risked the relationship with the person in the process.

Personally I think that the cutthroat type of business experience is a very damaging process for most people. When people get taken advantage of or cheated, they resent the person responsible for that treatment. Even if the people did something that caused them to be cheated, they still resented the person who cheated them. It's like purchasing a car and then finding out from a friend that they bought the same car from the same dealer and paid $5,000 less! How would you feel towards that dealer?

I approach every situation or negotiation in the following manner:

I find out what the other person or company needs and I also figure out what I want from the same arrangement. Then I go about trying to figure out how to make both myself and the other party happy with the outcome. I do not try to get the last cent or the most concessions from the other people. While I might make a few dollars more now, I damage long-term relationships later and that can be far more costly.

Throughout my career I had noticed that when something went bad and I would call people I had worked with in the past, they were almost always willing to step in and help out. Maybe it was finding a product in stock for me when it was in short supply or moving me to the head of the list when a tense situation was in play. Whatever the need, I was always able to get things done because others helped me.

But the people who always did their best to get the most or give the least in return always seemed to get polite excuses for why people couldn't help. They would say they tried but came up empty or some other excuse. I'm not sure if all of those replies were excuses but all I know is that I came through and they couldn't.

It happened far too often to be coincidences.

Over the years I created loyal relationships with people who always treated me well and made me aware of opportunities that most people never found out about. People always had my back and asked for nothing in return. They just wanted to be treated fairly and I always did that.

Granted I had several managers that would call me inside their offices and tell me that I could have got another $1 per unit or had a job done for $10 less and they told me to start being more aggressive. I would explain my approach and they would tell me that isn't how business works. They would tell me it has to be cutthroat because everyone is cutthroat.

The problem is that not everyone is cutthroat. There are a lot of good people out there who take care of each other and treat everyone fairly and watch out for their interests as well as their own. When the chips are down and your resources come through and help you save the day, hopefully then you manager will realize the value of what you were doing.

Some will but sadly some will not. But you know the truth and that should be all that really matters.

Don't Be Afraid to Take Risks

When it comes to advancing one's career that usually means bigger and better jobs. Along with those bigger and better jobs usually comes more responsibilities and more complicated or involved responsibilities. Sometimes we are hesitant to take those jobs, even when offered, because we either think we are not capable of doing them or that we are just not ready. Either way, when we turn down these positions for any reason, we stop the growth of our careers.

Most people fear the unknown and tend to makes things appear more difficult or complicated than they really are. The fact is, if you have the qualifications for a job and you have the intelligence to go along with it, you can probably do the job just fine after a training and learning period.

A lot of people fear failure and making mistakes as well and therefore do not take any better jobs until they feel 100% that they can be successful. Often times this means more courses, more studying and even more practical experience. While all of these are good things when it comes to improving our skills and capabilities, the problem lies when the person feels no matter what they do it is never enough.

This kind of career paralysis is quite common. It also effects other decisions in life as well. So we have to find a way to work around this and be ready to take the risks when they appear. Fortunately there are a couple of ways we can make ourselves feel better about applying for and accepting a new and better job.

Here are a few things you can do to reduce or eliminate the concern or fear:

Get the Information

Since fear of the unknown can be extremely powerful, learn as much as you can about the job. Ask people currently doing the job how they like it and what's involved. Read up on the position in trade journals or other sources. The more you can learn about the position the more comfortable you will feel heading into it.

Look at Others in the Job

Take a look at other people who are currently doing that job or had done it in the past. Chances are they were just like you and I and not super geniuses or world-class super heroes.

If you see people who are normal in every way having success in a job there should be no reason why you can't be successful as well.

Look Back at Previous Successes

Unless this is your first job you have already taken risks in accepting positions in your past and the results were probably pretty good. After all, you are looking to advance yourself now so you must be performing at a high level to be considered for the position. Feed off your past successes to give you confidence in tackling future challenges. You are more capable than you probably give yourself credit for.

Prepare Yourself Beforehand

Every job has qualifications and you should know and understand all of these well in advance. Your career plan should outline these qualifications and you should get as many of them in advance so you can feel comfortable and secure in your knowledge and capabilities. Getting and using advanced knowledge will not only make you look better in your current job but also make you more confident in your abilities in a new and better job,

Get Some Experience

Sometimes the best way to convince yourself that you can do something is to actually go out and see what's involved and try it out beforehand. Doing this allows you to get first-hand experience without taking much of a risk. You might be able to volunteer in that office or shadow someone to see what their job is really like. Maybe you can assist on a project with someone in that position and get some answers to some questions that will make you feel more prepared and relaxed.

Fear of the unknown quickly vanishes as you learn more and actually experience something. Once you actually do something and do it right, there is no more unknown. The unknown has been replaced by the known and your success will tell you all you need to know about your ability to do the job and do it well.

Think About the Worst

Though we should never dwell on the negative it sometimes helps to think about what is the worst that could happen if everything went wrong. Most of the time the consequences for taking a risk or making a mistake are nowhere near what your brain thinks they are. Remember back in high school when you were afraid to ask someone out because of the fear of rejection? That is the same thing. Had you realized that rejection then would not have been a really big deal you probably would have asked that person out if you never actually did. We all were rejected back then and most of us turned out just fine.

Think about what might happen if you would up unable to do the new job you just took. The worst that would happen is that you might lose your job. But chances are if you were good in your previous job and had a good work ethic you might just transition back into your old job. But even if that were not the case and you did lose your job, you would still have your family and friends and life would go on. You would just find a new job and start over. Millions of people have already done this and millions more will do so in the future.

One of the great abilities to possess is the ability to convince someone you are perfect for the job when you yourself are not so sure. But I have a little secret to share with you. Most people who apply for a better job have a little reservation about whether they know how to do the job or not. This response is completely normal and is no reason for concern. But what most people do is go ahead and tackle the challenge even though they have certain reservations.

In other words, they fake it until they make it. They go in and do what they know how to do and learn the rest on the fly. Maybe they work later because they take longer to do things in the beginning. Maybe they do more research or ask more questions or call someone who has the answers they need. They just do their best and learn as they go.

Almost everyone has some kind of learning curve in a new job. Management expects this and often has lower expectations from a new employee for the first month or so. During this time the new employee goes through the learning process and it is during this time that we act confidently on the outside even though we might be shaking in our boots on the inside!

You might even ask someone in a similar position in the company to mentor you or allow you to shadow them for a bit to get an idea of how the job is supposed to be done. You might even arrange to spend a day with that person before you start so that you can learn on your time and not the company's time. This could earn you a few points for initiative as well.

There is nothing wrong with "faking it until you can make it" as long as it doesn't place anyone at risk. For example, it would not be a great idea for a surgeon to fake an operation because he had never done one before. It also would not be a great idea for someone to sit behind the control of a commercial airliner and try to fly it for the first time with 300 people aboard. In other words, use common sense and take necessary precautions.

Do not allow a little fear or uncertainty to govern your actions. Everyone has a bit of fear inside and it is precisely this fear that helps keep us safe and protects us from doing stupid things. (Well, at least it should protect us!) The key is to keep fear it its natural place and not allow it to rule our lives and stifle our creativity and growth.

So go out there and take a few risks. Chances are you will do just fine and even if you do make a few mistakes you will learn from your mistakes and become better and stronger for it. Just don't do any operations or fly any jet liners until you're fully able to!

Create Balance in Your Life

We are getting to the end of the book and by this time I hope that the wheels in your head are spinning with all kinds of ideas and thoughts as to how you can make your career take off and how you can reach your goals faster and easier than you thought. At this point you might be excited and while that's great, let's discuss one thing that you need to consider as well when it comes to your career.

Your career, and the time and energy you devote to it, represent just a part of your life. Your career is not your full life and if it is, you need to take a step back and re-evaluate your life and priorities.

Make no mistake a good career that goes with a high paying job is important to a lot of people. But if getting that job takes away the rest of your life, it might not be a good trade off. Especially when there are usually ways of creating a great career and maintaining an active social life and family life as well.

You need to create a kind of balance in your life where attention is given not only to your career but also to your family, friends and other social activities. You must not always be too busy building your career to enjoy a dinner out or a movie with friends. You should not be so busy that you cannot go away for the weekend with a special someone for a little R&R.

This is not the same as being lazy or goofing off. What we are talking about is keeping a proper perspective on life so we can get to where we need to be safely and in a healthy manner. Our bodies need rest and downtime. Our brains need to tune out and relax a bit every once in a while. We need to laugh, sleep, relax and play so our bodies can calm down and facilitate the healing process.

Balance helps us attend to all the parts of our lives and also helps us reduce stress and anxiety as well. This enables our bodies to take care of itself and helps us stay healthy longer and better. Rest and relaxation also helps us "recharge our batteries" so we can resume work with renewed spirit, concentration and commitment.

If it makes you feel any better, people who rest and relax periodically are usually more productive and are able to think better and clearer than their "business only" counterparts. So if you are truly interested in building your career as quickly as possible you will take a few breaks along the way and spend time with family and friends as well.

After all, what good is a great career and a lot of money if you are all alone when you reach the top? Life is always better when you have good friends and family to spend it with. Think about that the next time you consider blowing off a dinner with friends to pull yet another all-nighter. Set your priorities right and don't make everything about business. You will life a longer, happier and much more fulfilling life when you create balance in that life.

Have & Be a Mentor

One thing I have realized over the years is that sometimes you get more out of something than you realize at the time. You realize days, weeks or even years later how something you did helped you in ways you never realized. Mentoring can be one of those things that can benefit you more than the person you are mentoring.

For those of you who do not know what mentoring is, mentoring is taking someone under your guidance and teaching them how to do something. You might take someone and show them how to build a home or hang sheetrock or write a novel or become a great salesperson or whatever your particular skill or talent might be. You don't have to be a doctor or lawyer or world-class expert in anything to be a mentor. All you need is the desire to teach or show someone something you already know.

A perfect example might be to take a new employee under your wing and show them how things work in the company and walk him or her through the basics and then be there whenever they have questions or experience trouble. Helping someone is always a good and noble thing to do and it can make a huge difference in that person's life. But it can also benefit you as well.

Mentoring someone requires that you know or understand something well enough to teach someone else how to do it. Being able to answer their questions often make you learn even more so not only are you improving their skills and knowledge but your own knowledge as well! This helps you become better at your job at the same time you are helping them become better at their job. It is a true definition of a win-win outcome!

I always believed that most everything in life goes better and easier when you have someone to show you how things are done and when you have someone that you can also pass down the information to as well. It's just one of those things that works out well for all concerned.

Mentoring others is also something that is appreciated and respected by others as well. Seeing someone willing to give up their time to teach and help someone else is a noble trait. It is just one more thing you can do to show others that you are a good person with a good work ethic who also believes in helping others and making this world a better place. I know that sounds a bit hokey but people respect those who take the time to mentor others.

Volunteer

Though we touched on this before a couple of times, volunteering in your community and within your industry helps accomplish a few important things. First of all it helps people and your industry while it also helps get you or your name out in front of more and more people. Since credibility and reputation often help immeasurably when it comes to landing a new job or advancing your career, this can be one of those win-win outcomes that usually help out everyone.

Second, it gives you a chance to get to meet people and find out what is important to them. If you are volunteering within your industry or neighborhood, this information can help you better serve your customers and your company.

Third, it exposes you to more people and lets more people get to know you. Since you never know who you will meet you will also never know where your next opportunity might come from.

You might just wind up working next to someone that might be your next boss or employer.

Fourth, it's just the right thing to do. Anytime you can give your time or knowledge to help someone else we should take advantage of it. I am sure you can look back in your own life and see a time or two when someone stepped up and helped you. It's just time for you to do the same.

Like many other suggestions in this book volunteering is just one tool you can use to become more well-known and become exposed to more different people. Volunteering, along with several other tips in this book will help you in your search for new and better opportunities and to help present yourself in the best possible way.

After all, opportunities often come when you least expect them and they sometimes come from places you had no idea existed. So why not take all the steps necessary to prepare your for the best of what comes your way? I think it just makes good sense to do just that.

Watch Out for Social Media and the Internet

Ten years ago there would have been no idea for a chapter like this and no thought given whatsoever to writing it. But over time things change and with the pervasiveness of the internet and social media, it is now time for some pretty frank discussions on the dangers of the internet and especially social media.

Most people, including myself and almost everyone reading this book, have done something stupid, offensive or maybe even illegal sometime in their past. For most of us, we might have several such events in our past somewhere. But there is a big difference between what we did 20, 30 or more years ago and what happens today.

When I was growing up and you did something you weren't supposed to be doing, the only people who knew were you and whoever was around when you did it and maybe eventually your parents. The exposure, and potential damage, was confined to just a small number of people. If the act was especially stupid, or done in public, then maybe the neighborhood found out.

But do something stupid today and someone is likely to capture it on a cell phone and post it on YouTube or Facebook and within minutes or hours millions of people might witness whatever it was that you did. As if that isn't bad enough there is another aspect of the internet and social media that is even worse!

When we did something stupid years ago, it was soon over and forgotten unless there were continued signs or reminders of what had happened. But if there weren't, people eventually forgot or they moved away or things just slid in obscurity.

But once something is posted online or uploaded to a website, it can stay there FOREVER! People can search for stuff that happened years ago and it is right there for everyone to see like it happened yesterday. Sometimes people might think something is funny while other times it can cause real pain and suffering to those involved.

As far as your career is concerned, you are in fact "selling" two things about yourself to current or prospective employers, you are selling your skills and knowledge and you are also selling your character and integrity.

Depending on the position you are applying for either of those two things could be the most important. But even for the least visible or important position personal character and integrity are very important.

Though many people might not be aware of this, almost every company is going to do some kind of internet check on your name at some point in the interview or evaluation process. Since this is so easy, this might even happen before you are invited in for an interview. You might make it through the initial screening and be selected for an interview pending the internet search.

So whenever someone type in the applicant's name, they see what is on the internet under that name. It might bring up a Facebook or Twitter page as well as any kind of post, article, website or any other entry for that name. The screener will then click on several of these links to see what there is about you online.

Let's say you are applying for a sale position in a very prestigious company with a very pristine image. You have all the right qualifications and excellent experience and references. You are a slam dunk for an interview and an odds-on favorite for the job.

But the internet shows pictures of you at a Spring Break party from 5 years ago groping some woman or you are a woman with topless phots from that same party. You are engaged is certain behaviors and it is all there in pictures and maybe a video or two.

How do you think the screener is going to feel about you after seeing these entries? Do you think these activities blend in well with the image of the company that is thinking about hiring you? Probably not and your chances for that interview are now slim to none.

Maybe there are blog posts you left with foul language or videos of you telling off-color or racist jokes. Or maybe there are posts on some off-color websites or worse out there all with your name on them. All out there for anyone to see.

And they don't go away, either. Not for a very loooooong, time.

At this point, you are probably aware of how this can severely damage any chances you have of getting anywhere near a decent job. If you think that we are exaggerating or that we are off-base, then that is your right to think that way. But if that is the case, do a bit of research in this on the internet. You will probably see a LOT of confirming information and articles that support what we just finished discussing. Even if you still think everyone else is wrong, isn't it worth a little effort just in the slight case we are right?

Here are a few things you can do to protect yourself from problems with the internet:

Search Yourself!

I do a search under my name and all my family member's names at least twice a year. I do this to see what is out there and make sure there have been no false or defamatory entries in the last few months.

Usually I do not find anything but one time I found an entry under my minor daughters name with some pretty vile and disgusting comments made in it. I was able to get that removed because it was posted by a minor about a minor and I threatened them with legal action.

This search takes about two minutes to do and can help you identify possible negative entries and also can help you discover possible identity theft as well. I think it is something that everyone should do at least twice a year. Do it more often is you start getting strange mail, e-mail or other warning signs that someone has assumed your identity or using your name under false pretenses.

Don't Do It!

If you are thinking about doing anything you would not be comfortable doing in front of your mother, father, grandmother, grandfather and your priest or minister, don't do it! The chances of some person seeing it and capturing it on their cell phone and uploading it are always there.

The best defense against having something negative posted or shared online is never doing it in the first place. That way you never have to worry about someone sharing something to get back at you or because they are jealous or whatever. If in doubt, just say "NO!"

Be Careful at ALL Times!

Unless you are inside your own home with the shades drawn and the windows closed, people can always see or hear you. That means someone can always shoot a video of you or record a conversation and share it with the world. It is not just videos that can get you in trouble. What you say, no matter the context or location, can get you in a world of trouble. If you disagree just ask any of the movie stars or television personalities or sports figures that said something they shouldn't that cost them their jobs or worse!

It is a sad commentary on society but you can never really be safe anymore these day from the eyes and prying of others. Everyone has their own mini television studio in their cell phones and people are all clamoring for their 15 seconds of fame even if it is at the expense of someone else.

If you think a co-worker or friend won't post something about you, think again. They might think it's hysterical but most people don't think for more than 4 seconds before they upload or share something. By that time it's too late.

Think 3 Times, Not Just Twice

Very often it is not friends or strangers that cause the problems but our own actions. We think that drunk picture of us on vacation is adorable and we just had to post it on social media. Or that person we woke up next too in the morning that we had no idea who it was? Perfect time to snap that selfie and post it on Facebook!

Maybe it wasn't a great idea to post that rant on the anti-gay website or come out with that Pro-Nazi diatribe on Twitter! Hey, it was all in good fun! Who cares!

The problem is that it is so easy to send an e-mail or post a picture or leave a comment that we often do these things without really thinking. Then, after we hit send, we have second thoughts. But by the time we hit send there was no turning back! The time to think, and think really hard, is BEFORE you type in the comment or e-mail and BEFORE you hit send! NOT AFTER!

Be Smart

Run everything through your "smart filter" before you type or post it. Think about how this particular comment or entry will look to people who do know you and who don't know you. If there is even the slightest chance that it makes you look bad or even suspect, don't do it. It is just not worth it.

Remember that these actions have consequences and that whatever you do today can be online and searchable for YEARS!! While writing this chapter I did a search under my name and found entries on the first two pages that were over 10 years old! So one stupid comment during a moment or weakness or emotion can follow you and haunt you for more than 10 years!

Do yourself a favor. Think carefully, run it through all the filters, and if there is any doubt, don't do it. There is just too much to risk and far too little to gain.

Remove Bad Entries

Removing a bad entry can be next to impossible. Since we all enjoy freedom of speech, we also enjoy a freedom of stupid which means that as long as something is accurate and truthful, it can be published without risk by the publisher. Which means if you really did have 10 margaritas and took your top of on the beach, that picture can remain on the internet.

You might have a shot if the entries were made about you when you were a minor or if they are inflammatory and untrue. You can try and contact the webmaster of the site who posted them but they may or may not listen to you. Even if they do listen you might have a hard time convincing them to remove the negative post, comment or picture. But it is worth a try.

Replace Bad with Good

If there are bad or negative entries under your name you might try and replace those bad entries with positive ones by posting some highly positive comments or pictures on some very popular websites so those entries show up on the first few pages and push the negative entries further back.

The though here is that most screeners might only look at the first 3 or 4 pages of entries and maybe not even that much during their search. Unless there are only a couple of candidates, they don't really have the time to go through 10 pages of results. However, for a really high level or important job with a lot of public exposure, they might go the 10 pages.

Get as much highly positive comments and posts so that they overwhelm the negative stuff and push it back further and further into the results. These positive entries will also help balance out some of the negative stuff especially if those entries weren't that bad and happened a long time ago.

After the Fact

If there are some things already online about your past, you are going to have to deal with them. I would first do all of the above things first to try and minimize the impact. But failing that, you are going to have to address them if they come up during interviews.

If they come up before the interview and they disqualify you there is little that you can do at that point. After all you do not want to bring them to anyone's attention pro-actively because there is always a chance that they won't find them or they will not think they are worth considering.

But if they do come up in an interview, do your best to explain them honestly and put a "spin on them" to make them look a little less bad than they really were. If these instances were in your youth you could say they were the result of youth and that you have grown up and matured now and hope that suffices.

Just approach them honestly and try to explain them to the best of your ability. Do not try to lie and say that it wasn't you (unless you have a common name and it REALLY wasn't you). These things are fairly ease to check out and you do not want to add dishonestly to your list of supposed crimes.

Whatever you do, do NOT take the internet and its impact on your chances of getting a job likely. The internet can help or hurt you a great deal and you do have significant impact on what is posted about you. While you cannot control the actions of others, you can control your actions.

By being careful not to do the things that people often video and post online, you can limit the negative fallout and the damage that follows. You cannot think you are immune or that someone will not video you and post it online. There are far too many instance of this already happening every day and they are only going to get more popular and happen more often in the future.

Conclusion

Your career is one of the most important parts of the majority of your life. The average person works approx. 40-45 years which is about half the time most of us are on this planet. Over this time we spent a lot of time working and trying to get more out of our lives and our careers. So it makes sense to commit ourselves to growth and excellence in our careers.

I hope this book has shed some light on certain things you can do to make your career and lives more successful. I say career and life because they are so closely intertwined that it is not possible to separate the two. You need to address both in order to be successful.

That is also why we stressed creating balance in your life as well. While your career is important so is the rest of your life and when you ignore everything in the pursuit of your career, you miss out on a lot in life in the process. So take care of your career but at the same time take care of your family and friends and social life as well.

The result will be a life that is full and enjoyable and successful. You will have money, success and people to enjoy it all with. Money and success without someone to enjoy it with is not really success at all. The problem is that many people discover this far too late in life. Don't be one of those people.

I hope that you got a lot of information and benefit from this "Hacks" book. It is one of what I hope will be many and I urge you to check back where you bought this book from to see the new titles as they come out.

Thanks again and good luck in your life and your career!

We Hope You Enjoyed
"Career Hacks"!

If you did, you might also
be interest in some of our
other "Hacks" titles!

Happy Hacks

Coming Soon:

Resume Hacks

Interview Hacks

Customer Service Hacks

Communication Hacks

Just go to wherever you purchased this
book to get all our other titles!